A Green Day

Embracing Climate Action

Jeevesh Gupta
Chittranjan Dubey
Anandajit Goswami

hachette
INDIA

First published in India in 2024 by Hachette India
(Registered name: Hachette Book Publishing India Pvt. Ltd)
An Hachette UK Company
www.hachetteindia.com

1

Cover design and illustrations by Harshavardhan Behura

ISBN 978-93-5731-975-1 (Print)
ISBN 978-93-5731-963-8 (eBook)

Hachette Book Publishing India Pvt. Ltd
4th/5th Floors, Corporate Centre,
Plot No. 94, Sector 44, Gurugram 122003, India

Typeset in Aldine401 BT 11.5/14.5
by InoSoft Systems, Noida

FSC www.fsc.org MIX Paper | Supporting responsible forestry FSC® C010615

Printed and bound in India by
Thomson Press India Limited.

A Green Day

Jeevesh Gupta is an environmentalist and social activist who works in the areas of disability and climate change. Jeevesh left his corporate career in 2010 and has been a social-change agent for over a decade. He has been a co-founder/active member of many groups and movements, including the Extinction Rebellion and Delhi Drum Circle and Movement to save more than fifty thousand trees in the seven GPRA colonies of Delhi. He runs a trust called Campaign for Differently Abled, whose motto is 'Let's see what they see and show them what we see'. He writes for a community magazine called *Samvada*, blogs actively on i-jeevesh.blogspot.com and is an active contributor to *Mainstream Weekly*.

Chittranjan Dubey is an environmentalist raising awareness about the ecological crises in Europe and India. His work has been covered by media houses like BBC, *The Telegraph*, Reuters, *Ouest-France*, *Reporterre*, RFI, *London Review of Books*, *TRT World*, *VICE*, *Bangkok Post*, *The Straits Times*, *The Economic Times*, *Times of India*, *Hindustan Times*. He volunteered with the Extinction Rebellion movement in cities like London, Berlin, Delhi, Brussels and Madrid, where people turned up on the streets, demanding their governments declare a climate emergency. As a social activist, he was involved in the India Against Corruption Movement in 2010–2011. He also teaches meditation in European countries in addition to his IT consulting job.

Anandajit Goswami is a research fellow with the Ashoka Centre for People-centric Energy Transition, Ashoka University, and has been a director and professor at the School of Behavioural and Social Sciences (SBSS), Manav Rachna International Institute of Research and Studies. He has been an ambassador of the anti-tobacco campaign of NADA Foundation across states and has been recognized by the All India Human Rights Council, Child Rights and You, and WWF India for his contribution in the space of human, child and animal rights in India.

Acknowledgements

We would like to thank our respective families and friends who have stood by us in our ongoing struggles to save Mother Earth. Many thanks to our book agent, Suhail Mathur at The Book Bakers for representing our book and having faith in our work. Thank you to the entire editing team at Hachette India for guiding us at each step. We would also like to express our deep gratitude to our contributors for allowing us to share their inspiring stories.

Contents

Foreword

M.C. Mehta

EARTH IS OUR ONLY HOME AND THE ONLY HABITABLE PLANET in our solar system. We have no plan B; we must nurture and protect what we have. I sometimes wonder how we miss the dreadful signs – the abnormal rains that cities are witnessing, the drought many regions of the world have been facing year after year or the rising sea levels, which will bring cities under water. These are not normal events.

In India, our constitution guarantees the Right of Life. Article 51-A(g), under the head of fundamental duties, places a duty on us to protect and improve the natural environment and have compassion for all living creatures. One must understand that the right may be enshrined in the Constitution, however, the enforcement of it is our responsibility – towards ourselves and towards our fellow citizens. Nature can only fulfil our needs, not our greed, as evidenced by the horrors that persist around us.

A heartbreaking reminder of such an atrocity is a small hamlet called Bichhri in Udaipur that has long suffered from groundwater contamination. The local acid-manufacturing and fertilizer industries continually pollute the nearby wells, resulting in scarcity of drinking water and compromised agricultural yield. When I first visited the place in 1989, I was appalled to see the villagers' fields and orchards damaged extensively, and the flesh of their cattle coming off the bone because they had to use the contaminated water day in and day out. I collected some samples from one of the water bodies and brought them straight to Delhi. The test showed that the water had turned carcinogenic. The toxic substances had been percolating deep into the bowels of the earth, polluting the aquifers and the sub-terrain supply.

I soon filed a public interest litigation. By then, I had been involved in a number of pollution lawsuits – including the oleum gas leak at Shriram Food and Fertiliser Industries in Delhi and the Ganga River Pollution Case. Getting an order was not easy, but the results of the contaminated water I had bottled during my visit helped me get a judgement in favour of the Bichhri residents.

When the hon'ble justice B.P. Jeevan Reddy inquired about the kind of chemicals mixing in the water, I placed the bottle of water in front of the judge and the opposing battery of lawyers. Some thought it was rum, but when they realized it was indeed the water that Bichhri residents had been using all along, they were surprised and started backing out immediately.

We got a judgement in our favour. However, despite the Supreme Court's orders, the sludge remained, and more poison continued to find its way into the groundwater. After a lot of to and fro, the Ministry of Environment, Forest and Climate Change was given the responsibility to remove the waste. Unfortunately, not much was achieved.

In a court case, the government, with the entire administrative system at its command, is on one side. The polluters, who are from the influential lot holding substantial power, can hire an entire army of lawyers. On the other side are an idealistic group of environment lovers seeking justice, with little knowledge of the technical issues, court procedures and scanty financial resources. Even when we are aware of our rights and duties, to take on the state and the vested interests of profiting parties is no easy task. The contest is invariably unequal. The court requires facts and evidence before it can gauge whether fundamental rights have been violated.

According to me, all of us should be environmentalists. There can be no better way to pay back to our planet. Some of India's landmark judgments in the environment space have been able to influence the global judiciary in favour of the greens. We need to unite globally to create a positive cross-border impact and stand against the polluters who are jeopardizing our planet.

Enforcement of law is the biggest challenge. During the British era, they did not let anyone touch the Aravallis or the water bodies right from Punjab to Delhi. What has changed now? Those who complain about the regulations – I call them the drawing-room warriors – say that our laws are weak, but they go silent when I ask them, 'When was the last time you enforced this weak law?'

Indian Council for Enviro-Legal Action v. Union of India (UOI) (1996)
M.C. Mehta v. Union of India (UOI) and Ors., Oleum Gas Leak Case, [AIR 1987 SC 965]
M.C. Mehta vs Union of India (UOI), Ganga Pollution Case [1987] 4 SCC 463

1

Jadav 'Molai' Payeng

Planting Life

Rituraj Phukan

WHEN AN UNASSUMING, MIDDLE-AGED MAN FROM A nondescript village near the Brahmaputra was conferred the honorific 'Forest Man of India' by the venerated Jawaharlal Nehru University on Earth Day in 2012, it was met with disbelief and awe. For most, this extraordinary honour came as a bolt from the blue, for Jadav Payeng was not a name known to many even in his home state of Assam. But for those who witnessed his single-minded devotion to tree plantation for over three decades, it was an expected outcome.

The extraordinary zeal is evident to the thousands of visitors who now flock to see the man and his forest. A decade after his forest was discovered, he continues to toil across the large swathes of sandbars that keep emerging every year after the floods. His efforts have led to greening the once desolate sandbars, which harbour numerous endangered and rare flora and fauna.

It wasn't until a herd of marauding elephants took it upon themselves to expose their long-term benefactor that Payeng's name was heard outside of his village. The story of 'Molaikathoni' (Molai's woods) thus began in 2008, with the pachyderms. The local media first heard of the man-made forest when some people referred to that spot as the likely refuge of the large herd. That year, for the first time, nearly a hundred elephants had ravaged Nauhotia thaan, Deurigaon and some *char* areas (river islands) of Kokilamukh.

'The herd had probably entered "Molaikathoni" from the north bank of the Brahmaputra and travelled further south to these mainland villages separated by another strand of the river,' the reports said. Some reporters followed up on the lead and found the man who had planted that magical wildlife abode in the middle of the mighty Brahmaputra.

When he was six or seven, young Molai (the nickname by which Jadav was known), was sent to stay with a Brahmin family at Dissoikash Bamungaon to get an education in return for helping with household chores. The decision to send the young boy was taken by his father, who was financially sound, at the behest of his son, for in those days, most of the schools had relocated to the mainland.

It must be mentioned that Arun Chapori and other islands nearby were once connected to the mainland. Arun Chapori is a large island where the Molaikathoni forest is located, and it has over a thousand human inhabitants.

Kokilamukh was a flourishing port and a major transport centre for Upper Assam. Then, the Brahmaputra changed its course, upturning the fortunes of Kokilamukh. Many families shifted to the mainland, but not Molai's father, the late Lakhiram Payeng, who chose to stay with his wife, the late Apholi Payeng, and seven sons to continue the family business of rearing cows and buffaloes and selling milk.

Molai stayed at the house of Anil Barthakur in Dissoikash Bamungaon, a village close to the city of Jorhat, and studied up to the tenth standard. His other nickname, 'Bamun', which is Brahmin in Assamese, was earned because of the genteel qualities he learned from his devout hosts during several years of living with them.

In 1979, when he was sixteen, the young man returned to his ancestral home in Arun Chapori, which was by then known as Borghup, or big islet. After some weeks, he left home alone to travel around in India and Nepal. When he returned, he resumed his studies but having failed to clear the matriculation exams, he decided to delve into the family business.

By then, his parents had shifted to Majuli, and his brothers followed them. Molai remembered his father telling him that the dry sandbar they lived on could be made more fertile by the dung of his livestock. Molai, who had decided not to join his family in Majuli, instead bought the livestock sold by his brothers and continued to live on the island.

He started selling milk – earning a reputation for good quality, his business flourished. Bipul Gogoi, a resident of the nearby village of Naohotia, and a friend of Molai, has seen the dry sandbar transform into a lush forest before his eyes. Bipul said that the young Molai would always seek out teachers, officers and village elders to talk with during his visits to the villages. Bipul also noticed that he would always return to the island with bamboo or other saplings at the end of the day.

In 1979, an incident occurred that had a profound effect on Molai and cemented his lifelong association with trees. He witnessed the painful death of over a hundred snakes that had been swept downstream during the floods and had met their end on the parched sands. It moved the impressionable young man to tears and further strengthened his resolve to plant trees. He would carry seeds and saplings from the mainland on his hand-rowed boat and plant them on the island. He realized that trees alone would not make a forest, so somewhere along the way, he even started carrying varieties of ants from the mainland. And for the next thirty years, he kept persevering every day, with few outside his close family and friends knowing about the lush forest he was creating.

Even today, he barely sleeps for more than three hours and often makes his way to the riverbank in the dark, paddling across the river to reach Arun Chapori by daybreak. After reaching the shore, Molai walks another five kilometres to reach his small farm in the middle of the forest. There he takes care of the livestock – cleaning, feeding and milking the animals. Planting or nurturing his trees, paddy fields or vegetable farms takes up the rest of his day.

In 2000, the Social Forestry department of Assam also started a plantation on Arun Chapori. Molai was at the forefront of this initiative, encouraging villagers to spare some land for plantation and reminding them of the correlations of the riparian community with nature. He himself donated a plot for plantation, and a cooperative of the villagers residing in Arun Chapori was formed, with his house serving as the office. He motivated others to join the efforts, pointing out that problems such as sunburn and poor eyesight that were prevalent in the community could be resolved by planting trees. One year, erosion displaced families from Majuli that were settled in Arun Chapori by the officials. However, protests by locals and the Social Forestry department forced the authorities to relocate the families elsewhere, and the forest was saved.

Bipul Gogoi, who cherished the 'sweet milky tea' served by Molai on his first visit to Arun Chapori, vouches for his dedication to the island community. Molai let go of a profitable fair-price shop that he had operated himself for two years. It is now run by others in parts across the island.

It is not clear when the elephant herds arrived on the island, but from the 1990's there were incidents of conflicts. After one such elephant depredation occurred in 2008, many local residents who had lost their houses turned against Molai. Some even wanted to cut down the forest that harboured the herds. Molai fought off all attempts at tree felling and asked the victims to approach the local legislator, forest officials and the Deputy Commissioner's office to solve their problem. For many years, Molai himself could not harvest the paddy he grew due to the rampage caused by the elephants. But unlike others, he shrugged it off and told everyone in Arun Chapori that they could sustain themselves by selling cotton, wild berries and vegetables.

He was so engrossed with his mission to green the region, that unlike most youth of his community, he resisted societal pressures to get married. He did get married finally, at the age of 40, to Binita Payeng and continued to live in Arun Chapori. For long, the family would be reprimanded by villagers for Molai's 'strange' obsession. Since Molai came into the spotlight, his wife Binita, daughter Munmuni and two sons, Sanjib and Sanjay, have been slowly coming to terms with the change in their fortunes. The family still remains rooted in their humble lifestyle and takes pride in ensuring that every visitor returns with good memories and a taste of the hospitality of their community.

Molai lived on Arun Chapori as long as he could, but the elephants forced him to shift his family to No. 1 Mishing Gaon at Spur No. 5, Kokilamukh, across the river from the island. He still has temporary dwellings on the island. The elephants seem to have taken a particular liking to his house and have damaged it several times since 2008. In recent times, family responsibilities and social commitments have made it difficult for him to split time between his beloved forest and his 'other' home on the mainland.

Once, he was asked to name three things he would get done if he were to be made the Chief Minister of Assam for a week. His answer was plantation, plantation and plantation. He went on to elaborate that firstly plantation would provide more fruit and seed-bearing trees that we need for dependent wildlife. Secondly, it would provide for firewood requirements. Lastly, he said with immense conviction that plantation of coconut trees all over the sandbars and on riverbanks would help to check erosion. 'Coconuts will also bring economic benefits to the impoverished inhabitants of these areas,' Molai explained.

'Besides, weaver birds like to build nests on coconut trees,' he added.

Molai continues to campaign for a forest office at Arun Chapori to ensure that 'Molaikathoni' is protected. 'The forest is now home to deer, buffaloes, tigers, elephants and in recent years, stray rhinos from Kaziranga. The personnel responsible for protecting the rhinos have a difficult time due to lack of any facilities at Arun Chapori, and a forest office will greatly alleviate their operational difficulties,' he said. 'I believe that these trees will one day alienate me from my fellow humans, as most of them are business-minded and would try to exploit these forests. My preventing them from cutting trees will cause conflict; another reason a forest office is now required.'

The 'Forest Man of India' refuses to be proud of his achievements as he believes in the creative power of nature. Ask him about his forest, and he will humbly tell you that his plantation efforts were supplemented by the wind, rainwater, livestock and wild animals, providing a lesson in seed dispersal he learned not in the classroom but practically on the field.

'Cows, birds, deer, elephants, are all endowed by nature to plant trees,' he says, 'but we humans know only to cut, yet we call ourselves supreme. Grasses and creepers have grown naturally, and I believe every human must protect the balance of nature. I pray to the Lord to give knowledge to the ignorant who are motivated by easy money to cut trees.' He has also said that he is happy to see the fruits of his labour during his lifetime and hopes that it would motivate others to take up tree plantation with the urgency it requires.

Molai is often seen in the role of an activist, calling out decisions hindering the conservation of the region's natural heritage. He has been critical of policy decisions, including the draft Environment Impact Assessment 2020, which would result in opening up of forest areas for resource exploitation, import of Australian grass to check erosion and other such measures.

'Assam would have been a desert by now if not for the tea plantations and protected areas,' he says, 'and since independence, we have destroyed much of our forest wealth.' He has also expressed his concern regarding the threat that unchecked population growth bears for the forests of the country.

In 2015, he was honoured with the Padma Shri, the fourth highest civilian award in India. Since then, his responsibilities and social engagements have multiplied. He honours every invitation sent by educational institutions to get a chance to interact with their students. He says, 'you can't teach an old myna to talk' and wants the government and civil society to focus on children. He has requested the government to introduce a policy asking every student to plant two saplings on their admission and nurture them through primary school.

Molai believes that the youth can and must bring about a 'green revolution' if the fortunes of the planet are to be turned around. He urges every civil-society organization to help him in his mission to restore the forest cover of his home state to at least thirty per cent of its total area. He believes the world can arrest catastrophic climate change by reforestation and has motivated thousands of men, women, and children to nurture Mother Earth back to health.

'A cup of tea served in winter, when the jhao grass dances to the clap of the kohua flowers with wagtails running around, with the sound of the Brahmaputra waters lapping at my feet and buffaloes lazing around in the morning sun, this is a magical feeling that cannot be replicated for me anywhere else,' Molai says, with an intense gaze embodying the motivation to keep toiling after all these years. These words of the 'Forest Man of India' will undoubtedly resonate with all visitors to 'Molaikathoni' for aeons to come.

Akila Kannadasan, 'Meet Jadav Payeng, India's Forest Man, who created 550 hectares of forest single-handedly', *The Hindu*, 21 March 2019. Last accessed on 27 March 2024. https://www.thehindu.com/sci-tech/energy-and-environment/meet-jadav-payeng-a-man-who-created-550-hectares-of-forest-single-handedly/article26589168.ece.

Manimugdha S. Sharma, 'JNU honours "forest man" on Earth Day', *Times of India*, 24 April 2012. Last accessed on 27 March 2024. https://timesofindia.indiatimes.com/city/delhi/jnu-honours-forest-man-on-earth-day/articleshow/12845235.cms.

'Social Forestry Wing', Government of Assam, Environment & Forest (website). Last accessed on 27 March 2024. https://forest.assam.gov.in/information-services/social-forestry.

2

Unlearn or Perish

Aseem Shrivastava

I WAS COMPLETING MY MASTER'S DEGREE IN ECONOMICS from Delhi School of Economics when the Bhopal Gas Tragedy happened. Over 3,700 people died immediately, and hundreds of thousands gravely suffered in one way or another. In fact, in 2020, many COVID-19-related deaths in Bhopal were of people who had to inhale the poisonous gas in 1984.

The disaster shook many people from my generation into wakefulness. The ecological perils of industrial society were much closer at hand than we had been taught to believe. Those of us who were trained in economics were particularly innocent of the imminent dangers.

After my master's degree, I took up a research assignment with the Centre for Science and Environment in New Delhi. I later proceeded to do a doctorate in environmental economics in Massachusetts. However, after my PhD,

I quit professional economics. My disillusionment with economics had to do with the stark unrealism of the profession in charge of a discipline vitally central to today's policy-making. One crucial aspect of the devotion to mathematically articulated fantasies in the name of high theory was that 'the environment' was treated as an 'externality', a belated afterthought to a technically rigorous study of markets. It was (and still is) understood as something 'out there', about which economists express their worry only secondarily, something which can be duly handled with taxes, quotas, permits and the like.

So, my first realization was that environmental economics just won't do. Too much of what happens to us (and within us) is umbilically connected with what happens to the world around us. For instance, the growing acidity of human bodies is ecologically rooted in the same forces that are causing the rapid acidification of the great oceans on earth. So, at the very least, economics had to become ecological, in the manner suggested by economists such as Herman Daly. It had to surrender its reductionist thinking about our living relationships with the natural world. It had to adopt a holistic mode of thought that wouldn't just reduce nature to matter (in the manner of science), and ultimately, to a mere 'resource' to be extracted and utilized for commercial purposes regardless of consequences for nature and human culture. The enormously costly triumph of this vision has meant that for most educated people around the world, forests just represent so much standing reserve of timber (or hidden minerals), and rivers imply water and energy. There is utter indifference towards their cycles of natural renewal. The sustainability of globally bloated commerce is rarely questioned in practice, no matter that pious lip service is paid to it everywhere.

After quitting economics, I taught philosophy, which had been a long-enduring passion for several years. Ultimately, I succeeded in marrying my ecological concerns with it, and now, for several years, I have been studying and teaching 'ecosophy'. It is a radically different discipline from environmentalism and even from ecological philosophy. Ecosophy can be loosely understood (in the words of the philosopher-theologian, Raimon Panikkar) as 'the wisdom of the earth', not our wisdom about the earth (which would be science). In my journey towards ecosophy, I have been significantly helped by Indian spiritual and ecological traditions. In particular, I owe a huge debt of gratitude to the teachings of Gandhi and Tagore. Equally, there has been much to learn from the actual living practices of Adivasi communities still very much in contact with the living natural world.

You have to unlearn a lot of modern intellect to look at nature afresh, listen to her rhythms, and understand how suicidally we are violating them. This has precipitated a global predicament that Panikkar describes as 'arrhythmia' using a medical metaphor.

With accelerating climate change and the rising frequency and intensity of extreme weather events, the sixth mass extinction, vanishing biodiversity, insect apocalypses, and unregulated population growth, this arrhythmia is all but terminal. Unless educated humanity wakes up to the burning house it inhabits and treats the coronavirus pandemic as a humbling opportunity to take pause and change course radically, our species' survival itself is at stake.

Meanwhile, many more such crises lie in store. This is how civilizations have perished in the past by losing touch with the rhythms of the cosmos.

The tragic aspect of our predicament today is that, globally, policy elites seem unable to perceive and comprehend the scale and imminence of the danger. Instead, they are busy with more parochial concerns such as accumulating corporate wealth to astronomical levels or growing nationalist power at the expense of nature and the human future.

The age of smartphones has ushered in a pyrrhic impatience in the war against nature. What is not understood at all is that the idea of 'the conquest of nature' is a vain myth, a rhetorical extension of a cultural pattern to nature, as every flood and cyclone painfully reminds us. The reason is that nobody can conquer the elements which work through nature, including our own neglected bodies, as COVID-19 has taught us. Every culture before modernity has worshipped the elements for this reason. It is the media-fed infantilization of our times, necessary to keep converting human beings into eternally restless, dissatisfied consumers, which sustains what philosophers would call a 'species solipsism'. Its dominant feature is that it confines privileged humanity to a seemingly comfortable, ever more digitized bubble, not allowing the force of the evidence of our collective crimes against nature and the future to cross over into the cognitive horizon of the public. It's too disturbing. So, the pacifying fable of technology (and the possibility of abandoning the earth in favour of another planet) is sold to everyone as the panacea for all the perils that await the future. There is much irony in the belief that this is supposed to be a 'brave new world'.

Perhaps more than any other country on the perceived high road to global glory, India has bitten the bait. Indian elites and aspirant classes wish for globalization's goodies no less than anyone else. But when it comes to guarding the interests of the future and conserving nature, little more than rosy rhetoric are served by those in power.

It is a tribute to the treacherous distance we have taken from the best in our traditions. The authorities think nothing of auctioning our vast ancient forest areas for the mining of coal or the broadening of Himalayan highways, imperilling in the process the ecological stability not merely of the great mountains but of the Indo-Gangetic watershed itself.

Pockets of our civilization were once rooted in the culture of celebrating and protecting forests. More than 14,000 sacred groves still here with us (not to be found in most of the Western world) are adequate testimony to this inheritance. The Upanishadic saying, *Vasudhaiva Kutumbakam* (the world is one family) was once a reality in large parts of the country.

Today, India is often just a clearing depot for timber and other natural resources. Those isolated communities, such as the many Adivasis, who are still in a position to serve as vanguards of the living natural world, are seen as 'backward' and are imperiously turfed out of their traditional habitats in the name of the nationalist adventure of 'development'. Quite apart from having (if only in principle) all the rights under the law, these communities could serve as 'early warning systems' for creeping ecological catastrophes in a world gravitating fatally towards metropolitan areas, which is where policy is made. Landscapes emptied of people will not have witnesses who could forewarn of troubles to come.

Besides, the knowledge of nature still available with the Adivasis has a broader significance beyond their own lives. When global drug and pharmaceutical corporations come bioprospecting to Asia, they poach (and later patent) much more from the traditional healers in our jungles than from government scientists. I recall a walk some years back in a jungle in Maharashtra, where a dozen of us 'educated' city-folk were given a tour of rainforest over several hours by a Phasephardi grandmother, who unknowingly made us feel ecologically illiterate next to her commanding knowledge of the herbs and plants we walked past.

I was once walking with a Santhal man towards his village in Jharkhand. Around dusk, he asked us to stop when we were still in the middle of a thick teak forest. I asked him how far we were from his home in the village. He responded, 'This is home.' Later I found out that we were some 500 yards away from his hut. For him, that was merely his 'bedroom'. The entire jungle constituted 'home' as far as he was concerned.

If there is still hope left in this country, it lies in the public recognition of the ecological wisdom of such people. We can still learn ecosophy from them. And this must translate into radical changes in the direction of economic and environmental policies. Far from this happening, the last people in the country who could teach us about ecological renewal and sustainability are being rendered superfluous by the ecocidal juggernaut of development. It is necessary to say that the days of folly are numbered.

Raimon Panikkar, *The Rhythm of Being* (New York: Orbis Books, 2010), 354-55.

———, *Cultural Disarmament* (Louisville, Kentucky: John Knox Press, 1995), 50.

K.C. Malhotra, Y. Ghokhale, S. Chatterjee and S. Srivastava, 'Cultural and Ecological Dimensions of Sacred Groves in India', INSA (New Delhi, 2001). Last accessed on 27 March 2024. https://wgbis.ces.iisc.ac.in/biodiversity/sahyadri_enews/newsletter/issue4/Yogesh_CEdimensions.pdf.

Madhav Gadgil, 'Sacred Groves: An Ancient Tradition of Nature Conservation', *Scientific American*, 01 December 2018. Last accessed on 27 March 2024. https://www.scientificamerican.com/article/sacred-groves-an-ancient-tradition-of-nature-conservation/.

Hannah Ellis-Petersen, '"Bhopal's tragedy has not stopped": the urban disaster still claiming lives 35 years on', *The Guardian*, 08 December 2019. Last accessed on 27 March 2024. https://www.theguardian.com/cities/2019/dec/08/bhopals-tragedy-has-not-stopped-the-urban-disaster-still-claiming-lives-35-years-on.

Pranab Chatterjee, 'Between Scylla and Charybdis: The COVID-19 Struggle of Bhopal Gas Tragedy Survivors', Pulitzer Center, 28 February 2024. Last accessed on 27 March 2024. https://pulitzercenter.org/projects/between-scylla-and-charybdis-covid-19-struggle-bhopal-gas-tragedy-survivors.

Jayashree Nandi, 'Coal blocks within dense forests find place in latest auction list', *The Hindustan Times*, 05 April 2023. Last accessed on 27 March 2024. https://www.hindustantimes.com/india-news/coal-blocks-within-dense-forests-find-place-in-latest-auction-list-101680633724811.html.

Jasjeev Gandhiok, 'CEC clears proposal to build roads in southern ridge near Delhi's Chhattarpur', *The Hindustan Times*, 16 December 2023. Last accessed on 27 March 2024. https://www.hindustantimes.com/cities/delhi-news/cec-clears-proposal-to-build-roads-in-southern-ridge-near-delhi-s-chhattarpur-101702662577692.html.

3

Adhitthana (Strong Determination)

Anand Reddy Yellu

HERE IS A DILEMMA. YOU SEE A CUTE BIRD, AND YOU SEE A cute child. Then, you see the child kill the bird with a slingshot. Will you punish the child?

Legally, we cannot punish children. The Indian Penal Code (or any other penal provisions) is not applicable to citizen under seven years of age. And morally, punishing a child for their lack of awareness didn't sit well with me. But the damage done by children with slingshots (*gulel/galor*) is significant and at times even ironical because they are destroying the environment of their own future. With all these limitations, the problem was eating away at me for months since my posting in Nashik.

Rolling back, my first posting after passing out from our training academy was in Nashik, Maharashtra. Apart from its pristine forests and being the location where River Godavari originates, Nashik in the Western Ghats is one of the two biodiversity hotspots in India. As a bird photographer who shot pictures of about 100 birds in our lovely Forest Research Institute campus in Dehradun, I couldn't wait to take charge as the Assistant Conservator of Forests, West Nashik Division. I was looking forward to going on field visits and capturing the wonderful birds of Nashik. But to my utter shock, the number of species I could see even in the interior tribal areas such as Barhe and Harsul was significantly low. Even the most common birds such as myna, robin and bulbul were rare to sight. Within a few months of field visits I realized that hunting of birds for food and sport using the slingshots was among the major causes of the decline of the bird population in many tribal talukas.

Though on the surface it doesn't seem like a big issue, the 'devil is in the details'. According to my preliminary survey in a few villages of Peth taluka of Nashik district, on an average 20 children per village were using slingshots to hunt, and 2 birds were being hunted per week by one user. Hence, an estimated 1,93,440 birds were being hunted in the 93 villages of Peth taluka alone in a year. There are 15 talukas in Nashik district, and there are 748 districts in India. You can do the maths. And the hunting is not restricted to just birds – slingshots are used to hunt small mammals, reptiles and some amphibians too.

The sad part is that the children (and most adults) are not aware that using slingshots to hunt is a punishable offence. Many patrolling staff have reported that adults would flaunt their slingshots with impunity even as uniformed guards pass by. I pondered for months to find some practical solution to this deep-rooted issue.

Two paths were already laid out. First was the well-established choice of ignoring the issue. And second, to prosecute the perpetrators as per law. While children cannot be prosecuted, even punishing adults under the law has limitations of scale and implementation in such community offences. Also, taking a legal course has negative ramifications as it disturbs the overall conservation paradigm of involving locals. So, we needed a win-win solution, one that change the attitude while also being sustainable.

But behavioural change is a slow process demanding time and patience. I chose the third path – to address the issue by its root cause. When lack of awareness lay behind an evil practice, how do we go about generating a sustained awareness? Our approach was to talk to each individual, tell them stories, convince them, make an appeal to change their attitude and incentivize their behavioural change.

Having no precedent and not knowing how the local Adivasis would receive the campaign, we started small. On 5 June 2021, using the platform of World Environment Day, Galor Samarpan Abhiyan was started in a small village called Adgaon, with the motto 'Galor Hatwa Pakshi Vachwa', to enable voluntary surrendering of slingshots. As many as 17 children came forward to surrender their slingshots. This was enough to motivate us to take the campaign forward.

However, what followed was something beyond our imagination. The campaign snowballed into a movement where it moved from child to child, village to village, until all 93 villages/padas of the taluka were covered in a span of 38 days. A total of 682 slingshots were surrendered. It should be mentioned that collecting slingshots was never our priority – it was merely symbolic as one may give it up today but get a new one tomorrow. Our target was to change the attitude of children towards slingshots.

In each village of Peth, we undertook awareness generation sessions to educate children (approximately 5,000) about the perils of slingshots. It was heartening to see children voluntarily reaching out to our staff and surrendering slingshots days after the session. In a few villages, certain children proactively convinced other children to surrender. These stories were indicators of the transformation we had been able to usher in.

Role of Campaign

As children and most adults weren't aware that hunting birds was a punishable offence, the main aim of the initiative was centred on attitude and behaviour change. For this, I relied on nudge theory.

Nudge theory is a concept in behavioural economics that proposes positive reinforcement and indirect suggestions as ways to influence the behaviour and decision-making of groups or individuals.

What were our positive reinforcements? Slingshot surrender was incentivized through immediate positive reinforcements such as colourful informational book on birds in Marathi, pens and entry into lucky draw with cycle, cricket-kit and volley-ball as prizes.

What were our indirect suggestions? For slingshot surrender meetings in villages we formulated a draft speech with reasons to save birds using ecological, cultural, legal and emotional perspectives. They were conveyed through short and simple stories/anecdotes in the local language. For example, the role of birds in the natural regeneration of trees was explained by asking children questions such as who do you think planted these mango/jamun/custard apple trees, the fruits of which we enjoy? An example of reasoning from an emotional perspective was how do you feel if someone hits your mother with a stone? You do not feel good, no? Imagine how birds feel when you hit with slingshots.

Children are fascinatingly open to facts and logic. Once convinced, they become crusaders of nature for a lifetime. Hence, it is important to catch them young, because a changed child is a changed generation.

Local Solutions to Climate Change

In the current scenario, no other issue is more crucial to sustainable development and global peace than climate change. And forests are a critical climate solution. Since the biodiversity that sustains them is increasingly under stress, the local actions taken today are a way forward to mitigate climate change. For this, the current conservation narrative should be broadened. We should start focusing on issues such as local biodiversity loss, pollution (especially plastic menace), slingshots, use of Chinese *manja*, forest fires, etc. Government policies indeed are steadily tilting towards these issues and the change could be catalysed through environmental campaigns. But policies and rules can only orient us in a direction, it takes the determination and contribution from each of us to reverse the damage that has been caused to nature.

Adhitthana in Pali language means 'strong determination'. And it is this quality that is required in all of us, from the first citizen of our country to the last citizen, from common man to the prime minister, from an industrialist to a daily wager. A strong determination is needed towards addressing at least one environmental issue that threatens our planet. In June 2020, children from Peth Taluka in Nashik pledged to never use slingshots.

The Indian Penal Code, 1860, s. 82, 83.

Sanjana Bhalerao, 'Forest officer makes children give up slingshots used to hurt birds', *The Indian Express*, 11 July 2021. Last accessed on 27 March 2024. https://indianexpress.com/article/cities/mumbai/forest-officer-makes-children-give-up-slingshots-used-to-hurt-birds-7398696/.

4

The Journey of an Environmentalist

Ashish Kothari

MY JOURNEY AS AN ENVIRONMENTALIST HAS BEEN A BIT LIKE looking into a kaleidoscope: the more you travel, turning new corners, the more shapes, colours and sequences you see. You realize that what you saw as a single picture has many dimensions, widths and depths.

It has now been over four decades, so memory is somewhat fuzzy, but I think my earliest interest in environmental issues started with animal rights. I was fond of animals and read something about horrible experimentation being done on monkeys. Around the same time, I joined the Nature Club in my school, attracted more by the fact that it took students out on trips than by the 'nature' part of it, but soon I got hooked onto birding and other forms of nature-related adventure. This is also when some of us in school or college 'discovered' the forest on Delhi Ridge, the last stretch of the Aravallis descending to the River Yamuna and began enjoying strolls through the unique green oasis.

It was a time of increasing news about ecological devastation: deforestation in the Himalayas, big dams on rivers threatening to drown out a rainforest such as Silent Valley and several wildlife species slipping towards extinction; and in our own backyard, increasing water and air pollution, and the destruction of the Ridge Forest for various urban projects.

My earliest involvements in the environmental movement space were actions against the export of monkeys to the USA (or rather, urging the then Prime Minister Morarji Desai not to re-open export), a demonstration outside the Saudi Arabian embassy against its princes coming to hunt floricans and bustards (just a dozen of us made enough noise to embarrass the Indian government into requesting the royals to go back), a cycle rally against pollution of the Yamuna and the horrendously smoky Indraprastha Power Station, and a rally against deforestation on the Ridge. Around this last one, which involved lots of school students (I was then finishing high school), we decided to set up Kalpavriksh as an organization that could regularly take up environmental action.

Then began a steep learning curve from the late 1970s to early 1980s, as we travelled to the Chipko Movement villages in Tehri Garhwal, visited mining sites in Goa against which the Goa Foundation and others were campaigning, studied impacts of thermal air pollution on a village near Delhi, carried out a spot investigation of police firing on villagers in Bharatpur National Park, and in 1983, took a fifty-day walking-busing-boating trip from the mouth to the origin of the Narmada river to look into impacts of the proposed mega-dam projects.

Why do I say it was a steep learning curve? Because it brought to my colleagues and me the understanding that environmental issues were also profoundly social, political, economic and cultural. Chipko's women were fighting deforestation and a patriarchal order in which men decided what was to be done with the area's trees. In supporting the protest of Molad Bund villagers against the Badarpur Power Station and visiting the mined-out craters in Goa, we understood the injustice of an economy that produces for the consumption of the urban rich at the cost of the poor. The complex issues brought up by our understanding of the Bharatpur incident brought home the shortsightedness and unfairness of top-down wildlife conservation policies that disadvantaged local communities. And the Narmada project drove home the biggest question of them all: what really is development?

In those early years, we spent time with people from movements and some of our elders already active in ecological and human rights issues as much as we could outside our study schedules. We learnt from the village women of Garhwal, from seasoned activists of Kerala Sasthra Sahithya Parishad, Sunderlal Bahuguna and Chandi Prasad Bhatt, Anupam Mishra, Vandana Shiva, Jayanta Bandyopadhyay, Claude Alvares, Ram Guha, the movement of traditional fishers against the commercialization of fisheries, movements against big dams in central India, and many others.

Of course, we continued learning from nature as a part of a research project at the Indian Institute of Public Administration. I travelled to many protected areas, and who can fail to be inspired by its many wonders (I retained a keen interest in birding, and immensely enjoyed writing the book *Birds in Our Lives*)?

I consider myself very lucky for having had these opportunities, not only because they gave me a wider, deeper, more nuanced perspective, but also because they gave me an orientation of combining activism and research, a grounding in issues of justice, an integration of human rights and respect for the rest of nature in their own right.

Fast forward to the last decade or so. In 2012, I wrote a book, *Churning the Earth: The Making of Global India* with Aseem Shrivastava. We analysed in great detail (over 300 pages) the ecological, social and economic costs of development in India, especially since 1991 when India moved towards globalization. Since then the pace of ecological devastation has accelerated, hard-fought environmental standards and laws have been systematically diluted or sidestepped, civil society spaces for participation in environmental governance have shrunk, nature-based livelihoods have been increasingly displaced or made unviable, inequality is rapidly increasing, and so on.

But we also wrote in the second part of the book about the radical alternatives that were emerging as a response to destructive development. A year or two before the book came out, I was already turning to a greater focus – on the question of not only what we are against, but what we are for. We say 'no' to mining, mega-dams, consumerism, etc., but what are we saying 'yes' to? What is our vision of a more just world? I'd started talking about 'radical ecological democracy',which we later labelled 'eco-swaraj' or 'Prakritik Swaraj'.

This has now been my journey over the last decade: the search for alternatives to the currently dominant system. To an extent, this has been a feature of all our work over four decades – in pushing for community-based and community-led conservation or advocating biologically diverse, sustainable farming based on examples we have known from various parts of India. I got a chance to go into such solutions more widely in coordinating India's National Biodiversity Strategy and Action Plan process in the early 2000s.

But it has been only in the last few years that this has become a predominant focus, with multiple dimensions and activities. This has included helping document and make known a diversity of alternative initiatives, especially in India but also some outside, beginning a process called Vikalp Sangam as a platform for sharing, collaboration, collective visioning and advocacy in India, and one called Global Tapestry of Alternatives to do the same at a global level, and in general, integrate the idea and practice of radical alternatives into neoliberal economic development, centralized governance, social injustice and ecological devastation.

In this, the main inspiration has remained the grounded struggles, innovations and joys of 'ordinary' people: Dalit women farmers of Deccan Development Society (DDS) who have overcome deep-rooted socio-cultural and economic marginalization to achieve food sovereignty and dignified livelihoods; Adivasis in central India who have taken back collective control over their forests and moved towards self-governance ('we are the government in our village': Mendha-Lekha village, Maharashtra); 'slum' colonies in Bhuj, Kachchh, who have organized themselves with civil society help to claim their right to the city and the planning of their neighbourhoods; and many more.

Over these last five to six years, we have put up over 1,500 stories of hope, resilience and innovation in India on the Vikalp Sangam and Radical Ecological Democracy websites.

From these experiences, we have also worked on radical and systemic change frameworks, developing something we like to call 'the flower of transformation'. This posits that fundamental change has to happen in four significant spheres of life: political, towards radical democracy or swaraj; economic, towards democratization of the means of production and consumption and bringing back relations of caring and sharing as the core; social, towards justice for all peoples and equality between genders, sexualities, ethnicities and moving towards caste-class free society; and cultural, towards respecting diversity and asserting knowledge to be in the commons.

Underpinning all this is, of course, the need to re-insert ourselves within nature (learning from indigenous and other communities that have always considered that they are part of and now owners of nature), respect its own right to thrive, and live within ecological limits.

And while we may look at life from these multiple spheres as an aid to understand the changes taking place, we also, of course, realize that real life is messier, more complex, more lived at the intersections between these spheres, and that the intersections themselves may sometimes conflict. At the core of this 'flower of transformation' are a set of values or ethical principles, such as solidarity, autonomy, rights and responsibilities, inclusivity, diversity, non-violence, love, the dignity of labour, and others, which are equally important. We can learn these values from successful initiatives of transformation and apply them in our own contexts, rather than trying to replicate or upscale those initiatives.

Because of this intricate and inextricable intersectionality, I have recently started talking about the need for a 'rainbow new deal' or recovery, not simply a 'green new deal' that is all the rage in the Global North right now. Pathways out of our global crises, including COVID-19–linked, have to be green, blue, red, pink, and of many other hues in that they must span ecological and social justice issues. Movements across the globe need to unite on these intersectional planes, respecting each other's priorities and seeing the complementarity amongst them, rather than the current territoriality and fragmentation we see. Perhaps the inspiring youth movements emerging in many parts of the world and on many issues (climate, peace and social justice) can achieve what their elders, people like me, have not yet been able to.

After forty years of struggle, many people ask me: With the ecological and social situation even worse than when I began my journey as an environmentalist, what makes me still hopeful? Well, it is pretty simple. I have seen 'victims' of destructive development projects themselves continue struggling, laughing and hoping that their actions will lead to a better life. I have seen that resistances can succeed (the women's movement, the anti-colonial struggles, etc.), and alternative initiatives can help transform lives (where would the Dalit women farmers of DDS be if someone had told them thirty years ago that it's all pointless?) even if the big wars are yet to be won. And I've been lucky to have had an excellent set of colleagues at Kalpavriksh (and the various other networks and groups mentioned throughout). So, what right do I have, I ask myself, to ever lose hope?

Ashish Kothari, *Birds in Our Lives*, (Universities Press, 2007).

Aseem Srivastava and Ashish Kothari, *Churning the Earth: The Making of Global India* (New Delhi: Penguin India, 2014).

Ashish Kothari, ed., *Pluriverse: A Post-Development Dictionary*, (New Delhi: Tulika Books in association with AuthorsUpFront, 2019).

Ashish Kothari, 'Radical Ecological Democracy: A Path Forward for India and Beyond', *Great Transition Initiative*, July 2014. Last accessed on 27 March 2024. https://greattransition.org/publication/radical-ecological-democracy-a-path-forward-for-india-and-beyond?highlight=WyJyYWRpY2FsIiwiZWNvbG9naWNhbCIsInJhZGljYWwgZWNvbG9naWNhbCJd.

'National Biodiversity Strategy and Action Plan', Kalpavriksh (website). Last accessed on 27 March 2024. https://kalpavriksh.org/our- work/conservation-livelihoods/nbsap/.

'Main Page', Global Tapestry of Alternatives (website). Last accessed on 27 March 2024. https://globaltapestryofalternatives.org.

'Home', Radical Ecology Democracy (website). Last accessed on 27 March 2024. https://www.radicalecologicaldemocracy.org.

'About Us', Vikalp Sangam (website). Last accessed on 22 March 2024. https://vikalpsangam.org/.

'The Search for Alternatives: Key Aspects and Principles', Vikalp Sangam (website). Last accessed on 22 March 2024. https://vikalpsangam.org/about/the-search-for-alternatives-key-aspects-and-principles/.

Ashish Kothari, 'Ecoswaraj: Towards a Green, Blue, Red Recovery for India', Slideshare (website), 24 June 2020. Last accessed on 22 March 2024. https://www.slideshare.net/AshishKothari6/ecoswaraj-towards-a-green-blue-red-recovery-for-india.

5

Green Hub Project

Leveraging the Power of Youth and Collaborations to Scale-up Ecologically Secure Futures

Rita Banerji

A GROUP OF TEN FRIENDS STUDYING IN DELHI MOVED TO A small town in Madhya Pradesh, in the drylands of India in 1991. Among them they held a mix of brilliance from different disciplines – economics, literature, science, design, sports and music. This area only had small and marginal farmers, dependent on rain-fed agriculture. Only one crop was sown in a year, and if the rain failed, there was no second option. Every year, it saw huge migration of village people to urban centres looking for daily-wage work. Money lending at 60 per cent interest, bonded labour and degraded land were only a few factors for debilitating poverty that existed here. Thirty years later, the same area has a company of 4,000 women members, benefiting 30,000 women farmers, who now sell and buy directly to the market. The farmers here grow two or three crops annually with the water table having risen over the years with watershed management. An enterprise of garments stitched by underprivileged women and people with disability, with a core team from the local area, has become a brand name. It took a small group of ten people – who could all comfortably get high-paying jobs in the city – to have that dream of working for the marginalized, working towards building rural India, with the true intention of redefining development. This ideology keeps community well-being and the value of ecological security at the core.

The group, on the other hand, started with one village in 1991 and have now spread over 574 villages and towns across the region. Working with partners, the company has transformed 72 of the most deprived districts in the central Indian Adivasi belt. This enthusiastic team comprises my family, my sister and her friends from college, and my parents who joined them soon after.

Against this backdrop, my work in the field of environment and wildlife filmmaking only helped to deepen the belief that ecological security is the foundation for community well-being and sustainable livelihoods. I think this is something that is understood largely by people. However, the overwhelming definition of development which is rooted in infrastructure, industry and urban growth continues to create a haze over the reality on the ground. The connection of natural systems to our daily survival – water, food, air – is not imbibed, the contribution of farmers to the national economy is ignored, and the work of people aimed at protecting forests and wilderness is seen as out of the box. The mainstream thinking around development still rests on urban expansion and industrialization, on huge profits and individual growth.

During our travels this was evident everywhere – whether it was turtle conservation, traditional livelihoods, honey hunters and the rock bees, protected areas and fringe villages, or community forests and indigenous people. Solutions existed everywhere, but the intention was missing. For the children and youth, while education is absolutely essential, it helps to connect them to their own roots, their own land. The narrative that defines success is moving to the city and getting a good job. I saw youth from fishing communities coming back to fishing after trying to get a job in the towns. I have seen youth here in north-east India returning after trying out different jobs in the metros. When they return home, there is a sense of being disheartened, a sense of failure. Ironically, they can identify plants, know the forests, can swim in deep sea, know their fish and nets and boats, but they do not deem these as inherent knowledge, as there is nothing within our education system that helps them to understand their own strengths. Youth forms 65 per cent of the population of India. How could we make them an asset for building an ecologically secure future?

Video is an incredible tool of learning and understanding. At the same time, it is also a way to document the incredible stories on the ground. Could we use this medium to engage the youth in conservation action and nature-based livelihood? Could we build a community of youth that is able to amplify the narrative around ecological security?

Green Hub Project was initiated with keeping these questions in mind. It is a video-based fellowship for youth, focussing on environment and wildlife conservation. We started in the north-east of India, across the eight states. And in 2021, expanded to central India. In the last eight years we have created a network of 200+ fellows across northeast and central India. Of these, almost 80 per cent continue to work on conservation-based or social-change projects through their own initiatives – filmmaking, working with NGOs and media houses, etc. While the tangible outcomes have been in terms of employment, grants and fellowships for community work, enterprise formations, the most valuable achievement has been the shift in attitude towards environment conservation. Many of the fellows who used to hunt now use their cameras to film wildlife instead. Many of them have realized the need to document the traditional knowledge and culture of their communities. There is pride in their roots, their own land, and also a sense of community with other fellows, and a belief that there is an avenue for livelihood that can be integrated with protection of natural resources.

The indicators for a paradigm shift towards a more balanced development model have been there now for a long time. Human-animal conflict is found in every corner of the country, but it does not come up in discussions when towns, cities, rural landscapes or coastal zones are being planned. Shortage of water in metros does not lead to protection of the source of water; disappearance of beaches does not lead to rejection of port proposals. And nothing can be bigger than the COVID-19, a pandemic which was a direct result of environment loss and degradation globally, and brought the world to a halt for two years.

In 2020, despite COVID-19 and the lockdown, youth from all across India, from all sectors, launched campaigns calling for the protection of natural spaces. Now there is much more consciousness about environment conservation and climate realities among the youth. It is time for us all to take a pause, reflect and listen to the young population. The future has to be aligned with protection of nature. There is no other path. We have the knowledge, we have the resources – it is time to collectively move towards a sustainable way of being, to scale up conservation and community well-being.

'Annual Report', Asia and the Pacific. UNFPA (website). Last accessed on 27 March 2024. https://www.unfpa.org/annual-report-2014.

'Home', Community: The Youth Collective (website). Last accessed on 22 March 2024. https://commutiny.in/.

Tushar Shara, 'The young environmental groups leading India's new climate activism', *The Caravan*, 15 March 2021. Last accessed on 22 March 2024. https://caravanmagazine.in/environment/the-young-environmental-groups-leading-india-new-climate-activism.

6

Proof of Concept

Raising Farmer Incomes and Environmental Sustainability

Mayank Gandhi

IT WAS 12 APRIL 2016. A TELEVISION NEWS CHANNEL WAS BLARING with the news: '12-year-old Yogita Desai, living in a small hamlet in Ashti, Beed district, in Marathwada, fainted and died while fetching drinking water. She had made many rounds to the handpump and the 44^{0}C sun finally got to her,' said the health officer. Along with the grieving parents and villagers, there were a multitude of little girls and boys, dressed in tatters, with deadpan faces and soulless eyes, staring at me through the television screen. It seemed as if they were living because they were not yet dead.

I prided myself at being stoic and immune to such tragedies, generally looking through these pain points with unseeing eyes. But that fateful night, I could not sleep.

The images haunted me every time I closed my eyes. Sleepless, I spent the entire night searching the internet for as many details as possible about the worrisome situation in Marathwada. The available information on the six droughts that had occurred in the previous eight years, the abject poverty, farmer suicides and the immense scars left by water and food scarcity on the psyche of the people, especially the young ones, really shook me up.

The summer of 2016 proved extremely challenging as the villages suffered from an acute water shortage. There was absolutely no water in the villages, not even to drink. I discussed the dire situation with Dr Wange, a noted surgeon practising in Parli town in Beed, Marathwada. After travelling across the villages with him, interacting with the villagers, spending time listening to families whose members had died by suicide, I started understanding the scale of this avoidable pain. It was heart-wrenching. As Immanuel Kant has said, 'You should do something, because it is the right thing to do.' Dedicating my life to make a change in the lives of these farmers seemed the right thing to do. I instantly made the decision to spend the rest of my life working towards transforming the country by creating a crucible of change, beginning with Marathwada.

To immediately address the water shortage issue in the region, as an emergency measure, water tankers were supplied to 56 parched villages, financed through crowd funding till the monsoon arrived. Interactions with more and more villagers continued, with the quest to try and understand the ongoing scenario and the grievances. The climate crisis was making every year worse than the earlier ones. This was no longer academic knowledge for me, it was *real*, palpable and unfolding in front of my own eyes. It was clear that the worsening climate and geographical conditions were majorly impacting the poorest and the most vulnerable in India's villages. It was time to roll up one's sleeves and start working.

The two biggest problems that needed to be tackled head-on were poverty and the climate crisis. After selling my home in the city, I started living in the villages. The aim was to try and generate an initial interest about the possibility of transforming lives through collective action among the stakeholders. The underlying hope was that this would eventually lead to people's participation in a pro-development and non-confrontational movement. The Global Vikas Trust (2016) was thus born, its objective being to stir a mass movement in order to enhance farmer incomes and enrich the natural environment through the extensive plantation of millions of fruit-bearing trees.

Despite my best efforts, the progress of the movement in the beginning did not align with my expectations. Although our meetings drew hundreds of inspired villagers, there was a noticeable absence of female participation. Without women, there certainly cannot be a movement. Our relentless attempts to encourage the village women proved futile as the deeply entrenched patriarchal norms prevented them from attending such gatherings.

It was in the latter part of 2017 that a miracle happened. I was addressing a small temple meeting in a little village called Rewali. While I was speaking in broken Marathi, someone in an inebriated state from the gathering started speaking louder than me. Irritated, I said, 'At least do not drink and come to the temple.' After the meeting, I felt that maybe I should not have publicly humiliated the concerned person. But the sarpanch took this episode very seriously. He, along with a few senior villagers, approached the local illegal hooch shopkeeper and told him, 'Already seven youth in the village have died of cirrhosis of liver due to over-drinking. In the evening, drunk men sleep on the roads. Women and even 10-year-olds have started drinking. Why don't you stop selling alcohol?'

I have no idea what happened and how it happened, but change did occur. The shopkeeper said, 'I have seven days of liquor stock, let me finish that and I will stop.' The sarpanch called me and informed me of the development. Elated, I rushed the next morning to the shop, caught the feet of the shopkeeper and told him, 'God has come within you. Now, how will you look after your family? Let me give you three pregnant goats so that you can earn an income through goat rearing.' After seven days, he stopped selling liquor, and I gave him the three pregnant goats, and from there started a unique movement.

With the help of the villagers and the local police, we started raiding various liquor shops. The menfolk would run away, and I would hold the feet of the lady of the house and plead, 'Mother, as long as I am there, these raids will not stop. Why don't you stop selling this illegal liquor, and I will give you three pregnant goats?' It worked. At night, the youth and women would carry burning *mashaal*s (torches) and go through village after village shouting, 'No liquor will be allowed.' Women would sit outside liquor shops chanting the name of Lord Rama. In fifteen days, the movement became an undeniable success. All the liquor sale points stopped, while we gave the shopkeepers three pregnant goats each.

Although many of those addicted to alcohol went to far-away villages to drink, the overall incidents of drinking reduced. My public meetings would see rows of women listening and proffering their support. Revolutionary songs found their way into our programmes. A movement was on its way.

The summer of 2018 was scorching. The land was dry but the spark in the eyes of the villagers excited me. It was as if something special was waiting to happen. Where there was earlier hopelessness, now lay enthusiasm and determination. They had tasted the flavour of success by working together. We had to take advantage of the mood.

In the sweltering days between 15 April 2018 and 31 May 2018, we rallied fifteen villages together with the resolute purpose of fighting the drought in forty-five days. Starting from 5:30 a.m. in the morning every day, armed with proper tools and in a well-planned manner, we started digging rivers, ponds and trenches till 1.30 a.m. the next morning. A break was taken in the sweltering afternoon. Machines were rented and men and women worked together as if possessed. The final outcome was 70 kms of deepening and widening of the Paapanashi river and its tributaries – 162 farm ponds, 62 check dams, 5 KT weirs, hundreds of trenches and 222 crore litres of water storage created in just 45 days. Change was well on its way.

And then the rains came, and soon the place was buzzing – with the green cover serving as a vital source of sustenance for countless microorganisms, insects, birds and animals, while also contributing to the increased production of oxygen.

Hope replaced hopelessness. Green had replaced brown. Life replaced barrenness.

It was time for the biggest gamble. And this is how it unfolded.

In the usual course, farmers were engaged in cultivating cotton and soya crops, yielding an annual income of approximately Rs 25,000 per acre. With a deep commitment our team embarked on a journey, visiting one village after another with the aim of persuading farmers through factual information, figures and statistical data to consider a shift in their cropping choices towards fruit-bearing trees, which would in turn boost their earnings. Despite having established trust and affection within the village communities over the years, the farmers somehow remained reluctant to depart from their traditional cropping patterns.

In 2019, we were able to convince 1,700 farmers to change their crops to horticulture and plant 1.18 million fruit trees. In 2020 and 2021, in spite of COVID-19, the farmers planted 1.9 million and 7.8 million trees, respectively. In 2022, the farmers planted 21 million trees and in 2024, we hope to plant 35 million more. Short-term trees such as banana and papaya, medium-term fruit trees such as custard apple, guava, pomegranate, lemon, sweet lime and mosambi, and long-life trees such as mango increased farmer annual incomes from Rs 25–50,000 per acre to an average of Rs 2,50,000. Our highly successful 'proof of concept' slowly started attaining traction among the farmers and has expanded to 2,900 villages in 29 clusters in Maharashtra and Madhya Pradesh. This initiative and the resultant change has led to the total plantation of over 40 million trees.

The increase in green cover through large-scale tree plantations not only induced remarkable rainfall but also transformed a once-drought-hit arid area into a flourishing expanse of greenery. A significant outcome has also been the enhanced participation of all stakeholders involved in the endeavour, fostering a sense of collective responsibility.

The revival of rural prosperity is imperative as over two-thirds of India resides rurally. The Global Vikas Trust's objectives are to harness the power of green cover, notably through extensive tree planting, bolstering rural incomes, fostering environmental sustainability and contributing to the broader vision of uplifting the incomes of the rural farmers.

Heather Wilburn, 'An Introduction to Kant's Moral Theory' (Oklahoma: OpenOKState, 2020).

Shoumojit Banerjee, 'Water experts warn of "desertification" of Marathwada', *The Hindu*, 23 March 2019. Last accessed on 22 March 2024. https://www.thehindu.com/news/national/other-states/water-experts-warn-of-desertification-of-marathwada/article27212356.ece.

Press Trust of India, '2018 Summer: "Above Normal" Temperatures Between April-June', NDTV, 02 April 2018. Last accessed on 22 March 2024. https://www.ndtv.com/india-news/2018-summer-above-normal-temperatures-between-april-june-1831494.

'Home', Global Vikas Trust (website). Last accessed on 27 March 2024. https://www.globalvikastrust.org/index.html.

7

Impact of Climate Change on Health

Youth Advocacy – I

Karina Weinstein, Adrienne Dean,
Annika Johnson and Jack Feinberg

'The health of our children depends on urgent climate action.'

WHEN MY THREE-YEAR-OLD SON CAME HOME FROM CAMP VERY ill, I knew that his asthma was exacerbated by his exposure to the extreme heat. It has been widely documented that burning fossil fuels leads to climate change and increases air pollution, which increases the risk of asthma – especially in children. My commitment to addressing the climate crisis stems from raising two children with childhood asthma and seeing its disruptive consequences on their lives, especially during a time when the climate is changing so rapidly. I always have to be very deliberate in how my kids engage in activities during the extreme heat or the extreme cold, knowing that both scenarios can lead to debilitating asthma attacks. I have experienced first-hand how climate change impacts our health, and how it is not only an environmental crisis, but also a public health crisis.

In leading the FXB Climate Advocates programme – a global climate advocacy youth network – I am constantly inspired and awed by high school students' focus on climate solutions and by their determination to address the climate crisis in real time. The FXB Climate Advocates programme informs, empowers and mobilizes youth to act on the climate emergency by facilitating access to resources and networks. This programme is designed to equip youth climate activists with the tools to mobilize climate action on a local, national and international level. In spite of the anxiety youth feel about the devastating impacts of climate change, they are constructive and proactive in advocating for climate solutions.

Participants of FXB Climate Advocates programme are developing cooling centres, reducing electricity usage in schools, starting municipal composting initiatives, leveraging artificial intelligence for climate advocacy, and replacing Styrofoam with sustainable reusable plastics in large school districts, and other such climate advocacy initiatives. Through the Liveable Cities Committee and the Climate & Health Advocacy Track, FXB climate advocates are learning about the connection between climate and health, the burden experienced by the most vulnerable communities in the US and globally and existing initiatives that improve people's health.

FXB USA approaches its work with youth climate leaders through two key frameworks: focusing on climate solutions and supporting students to select advocacy strategies that resonate with them. The focus on climate solutions promotes agency in our students. The world knows what needs to be done to address the climate crisis, but doing so is a matter of mobilizing people and necessary resources. The second aspect of our programme's strategy is that rather than dictate how students should get involved to address the climate crisis, we support them to chart their own climate journeys and identify advocacy strategies that are aligned with their skills and interests.

From the students we have served through our programme, I learned that many of them connect with climate advocacy through environmentalism and sustainability, focusing on actions such as making more sustainable consumption choices and protecting the natural world. With no compulsory and comprehensive climate and environmental literacy in schools in the US and around the world, students are left to fend for themselves to seek knowledge about climate change and identify pathways to take action. Besides an environmental science course, many schools do not offer education on the most pressing issue of our time. While students are not formally taught about the connection between climate and health, they are feeling the consequences of the impact of climate change on health first-hand.

As an organization that coaches and guides climate activists to implement climate solutions, FXB USA intentionally selected the connection between climate and health as one of our core focus areas. One of the programme's key goals is for students to understand how climate change is a public health issue. The connection between climate change and health is not one that most youth climate advocates are exposed to through school curriculum or extra-curricular sustainability/environmental activities. FXB USA believes that climate solutions must protect not only the natural world, but also improve people's health, so that they can lead prosperous lives. This approach is the embodiment of FXB's vision which seeks to help the most vulnerable people around the world not only to survive but to thrive.

The focus on climate and health as part of the FXB Climate Advocates programme enables students to break down the seemingly daunting issue of climate change and feel that they have agency to make an impact on their communities. While students may not have much control over carbon emissions from buildings or transportation, they can play a critical role in advocating for climate-change mitigation and adaptation efforts in their communities that enhance people's health. By starting out with a focus on their own communities, students gain understanding of climate change, how it is impacting their communities and the different stakeholders involved in addressing the different impacts. In exploring how climate change and health are connected, students can reflect on their lived experiences which in turn enriches their climate advocacy. Our long-term goal is for participants of FXB Climate Advocates programme to advocate for a clean-energy economy and protect the most vulnerable communities from the impacts of climate change.

FXB is an international development organization that works to create a world where everyone has a chance not just to survive but to thrive. FXB's mission is to provide the poorest of the poor families with the tools and support they need to become self-sufficient and give their children a better future.

FXB helps implement lasting change in the countries where it operates through a multidimensional response to poverty, implementing programmes that simultaneously address economic empowerment, nutrition, housing, education, and health. All of FXB's actions focus on realizing children's rights and contribute to the objectives set by the UN Sustainable Development Goals, while bringing to life its vision of a world without poverty. Thanks to a rigorous methodology focused on children's rights and empowerment, FXB gives participants the tools to become socially and economically independent so that they can support themselves and offer a brighter future to their children.

FXB is a global organization with over 30 years of experience in lifting vulnerable communities out of poverty. FXB has been addressing pressing societal challenges such as children's and women's rights and climate change since its inception. The concern for the environment as it intersects with health is at the core of the pioneering FXB Village Model – a holistic intervention that has lifted over 1,00,000 people out of extreme poverty in ten countries. Since its founding in 1989, FXB has served 18 countries, resulting in 18 million adults and children benefiting from its presence in their communities. FXB is currently implementing programmes in 13 countries: Burundi, France, Gaza,

India, Mongolia, Myanmar, Namibia, Niger, Rwanda, South Africa, Switzerland, Uganda and the United States.

FXB was founded with the mission to implement the Articles of the Convention on the Rights of the Child as these directly concern children orphaned by and infected with HIV/AIDS. Over time, FXB expanded its work to include families and children affected by multiple causes of vulnerability, including conflict and poverty.

'Through its far-reaching impact on all parts of society, climate change will challenge the very essence of children's rights to survival, good health, well-being, education and nutrition as enshrined by the Convention on the Rights of the Child and emphasized in the UN Sustainable Development Goals.' Climate change is an imminent threat to children's health and well-being and their ability to exercise the rights delineated in the Convention on the Rights of the Child.

As a child rights organization, the SDG 13 on climate action is a key priority for FXB as we continue to empower communities around the world to overcome poverty, live a dignified life and provide a brighter future for their children.

– by *Karina Weinstein, Programme Strategy and Innovation Director, FXB USA*

Curriculum tailored to needs

It was my pursuit of a career in medicine as a physician that first introduced me to the world of public health and my interest in climate-health advocacy. I have always been interested in political activism, particularly in my own communities in the US. Before attending medical school, I decided to pursue a degree in public health to study how society promotes and protects our health globally. Climate change is one of the largest threats to global health, and much of the general population is only vaguely aware of its health implications. As a master of public health student and future physician, I set on the challenge to learn about how climate change is impacting human health and what can be done to mitigate its effects.

The impact climate change has on health is broad and extreme. It endangers respiratory and cardiovascular health, mental health and food stability; increases water-borne illnesses; and threatens lives with extreme weather events. The impact of climate change on health is an issue of environmental and social justice. Societal factors such as poverty, discrimination, access to healthcare and pre-existing conditions make some populations more vulnerable than others. Adrienne Hollis, a lead climate analyst at the Union of Concerned Scientists, explained in *TIME* that as climate change continues to alter disease patterns and disrupt health systems, its effect on human health will become harder to ignore. It needs to be addressed by policy change at the local and international level. While the causes of climate change occur globally, the health impacts are local. This relay of climate facts – that we hear on the news and in our daily lives – can create anxiety for many, resulting in even more stress on mental health. However, it's important to know the issue so we can address it. The solution to climate anxiety is action.

Broad public participation is necessary to combat climate change. Both children and adults need to participate in climate-change efforts. The children born today are unique in that they will be the first generation whose entire lifespan will be impacted by climate change. Not only that, children and youth are among the worst affected by climate change. Children – because of their unique developmental characteristics and life expectancy – are more vulnerable than adults to the effects of climate change. As awareness grows and the impact of climate change is becoming more severe, children and young people are taking action. Youth around the world are already actively addressing climate change by raising awareness locally and online, organizing projects in their communities and promoting use of renewable energy. An important component of children's health is agency. Taking action can help the youth feel more in control, more hopeful and more resilient.

I participated in the NYU Urban Health Lab through which I connected with FXB USA to support the Liveable Cities Committee as part of the FXB Climate Advocates programme. I collaborated with Karina Weinstein, who leads the programme, to address the obstacles faced by youth in their climate-action efforts. In a 2012 study led by Dr Sonia Brondi of University of Padova, reasons for youth disengagement included 'the perception that no initiatives had been organized or that they had been inadequately promoted; then, the perception that they are too young to do anything and would rather delegate to others (adults, experts etc); and finally, a sense of powerlessness and resignation.' Many youth projects are also short-term and focus on issue-specific activism. Not all forms of climate change activism are created equal. Youth may not know what they are capable of achieving. With adult guidance, youth advocates can be empowered through training, building a knowledge base, and practising skills and behaviours that will improve the health of their community through direct action.

I worked with FXB to create a curriculum and guided research projects to prepare and support youth to become climate-health advocates. I define climate-health advocates as those who seek mitigation and adaptation against the immediate and long-term harmful effects of climate change on human health. The goal of this guided approach was to provide students with information on climate science and public health so that they may learn about climate threats that affect health in their local communities. Students conducted a research project to address the impact climate change has had on health in their communities by developing and implementing an intervention to mitigate its impact and improve health outcomes. Each student examined the impact of climate change on health in their nearest city, proposed an intervention for transforming the built environment and presented that intervention to state or community councils.

Annika Johnson, a student from Massachusetts, created a project to battle rising temperatures and the urban heat island effect in East Boston. The goal was to implement pocket-parks, increase canopy cover and improve access to outdoor cooling, such as battery-powered misting systems.

Another student, Jack Feinberg from New York, worked on a project to improve air quality and green space in the Bronx, New York City. After learning that American sweetgums are one of the best tree species for absorbing and storing carbon dioxide, his goal was to increase the percentage of these trees planted in the Bronx to provide more green space to neighbourhoods and improve air quality.

Promoting youth engagement through this curriculum and guided research project improved climate change mitigation efforts through improved community building and 'improve[d] sustainability of initiatives on climate change.' Guidance on individual student projects and curriculum supported students into becoming active citizens, giving them the opportunity to identify and discuss environmental problems. It promoted active participation by connecting them to solutions, and ultimately preparing them to be climate advocates.

– by *Adrienne Dean, MPH Student, Icahn School of Medicine at Mount Sinai*

Small Steps. Major Implications.

Like many young people who are acutely aware of the danger and urgency of climate change, I often struggle with a sense of powerlessness against this massive, amorphous issue that I know I will see the impacts of in my lifetime. In fact, in recent years, I have noticed such consequences arising in my own hometown, from heat waves to extreme storms.

I sought out the FXB Climate Advocates programme partially to combat this fear. It's reassuring to know that so many people, both in the programme itself and FXB's robust network of connections, are fighting climate change, and it's empowering to promote large-scale sustainability with like-minded teens across the country.

FXB has provided me with the knowledge, skills and resources to become a more effective climate advocate. Hearing from expert speakers, attending educational sessions and being encouraged to do my own research, I have gained an understanding of the many complexities of the climate crisis. Climate change seems like a simple problem to understand, but FXB exposed me to its intricacies and intersections with other fields, from agriculture to systemic racism.

Beyond this, I became fluent enough in many of these issues to educate others through FXB and was provided multiple opportunities to present at events such as a Forum 2100 webinar (research initiative focused on energy) and the International Conference on Urban Health. I honed my presentational skills and learned to appeal to my audience, explaining the importance of environmentalism in specific fields.

Joining the FXB Climate Advocates programme also gave me perspective on how to address climate change through seemingly small steps with major implications. As I mentioned, maintaining one's passion for environmentalism when confronted with climate change as an enormous, existential issue with infinite complexities can be difficult. However, FXB helped me understand climate change as an umbrella term, to identify specific areas within sustainability that I'm passionate about and to break these fields down further to set specific, achievable goals. This support was crucial to change-making in my community, because moving past fear and identifying an issue that I was passionate about *and* that I could address was the essential first step in my work.

The issue that I eventually chose to fight against was the effect of climate change on public health, and I was able to do so through FXB's Liveable Cities Committee. I decided to join this committee because I believe the intersection between climate change and public health must be explored more deeply; not only is climate change already a major health threat for vulnerable communities, but exposing this fact could also be powerful in mobilizing the population in support of sustainable change. I also appreciated that this committee was focused on environmental justice. Unfortunately, racial and socioeconomic inequality are embedded in virtually every issue, including climate change. A committee dedicated to bettering health and quality of life in urban areas would have to acknowledge this reality, and I knew that I wanted to focus on intersectionality and the US's unjust history within my climate work.

With the Liveable Cities Committee, I researched the most prevalent climate and health threats to my state of Massachusetts. I eventually chose to focus on elevated heat. I quickly identified East Boston as a particularly vulnerable neighbourhood. East Boston is home to Boston Logan International Airport, an affluent community along the waterfront, and blocks of working-class families battling the heat. East Boston is uniquely sensitive to heat due to the urban heat island effect (which exacerbates elevated temperatures in cities), lack of air conditioning, high instances of diabetes and unequally distributed canopy cover. It is also essential to note that the most sensitive areas within East Boston itself are majority Latin communities, who have likely been subject to a long history of planning and medical injustices that led to their current struggle against elevated heat.

Adrienne Dean, member of the NYU Urban Health Lab and MPH candidate from the Icahn School of Medicine at Mount Sinai, guided me through my research, helping me to construct a clear narrative that connected Massachusetts's rising temperatures and East Boston's social determinants of health to potential for major health impacts, including heat-related illness, exacerbation of cardiovascular and respiratory illness and the shockingly high death rates due to heat waves.

From here, I designed an intervention that aimed to combat elevated heat from multiple angles and adjust to criticisms of existing adaptation strategies. My idea was to combine two existing strategies: greening and use of cooling centres in pocket parks using cooling devices. The greening spaces would increase canopy cover, which has marked cooling effects, and pair with devices such as misters to provide refuge from extreme heat while also providing CO_2 absorption from trees. This combination felt so logical to me that I was shocked that it was not already being implemented, especially considering the fact that Boston's existing cooling centres, in spaces such as libraries, were underused and inaccessible. Many residents felt uncomfortable in these spaces, especially undocumented immigrants prone to uneasiness around seemingly official buildings. I hoped to create a more informal space that would offer not only cooling, but also ensure that it was taken advantage of.

I had the opportunity to communicate with many stakeholders, from Boston-based nonprofits and members of the Metropolitan Area Planning Council's Public Health Department to a project manager with Boston's heat response planning team. These experts allowed me to promote my intervention and offered inputs on how it could be implemented, including partnership with local businesses. One of my most memorable experiences from this process was attending an Idea Session on heat adaptation in East Boston, held by the city of Boston. I was incredibly grateful for the opportunity to contribute my ideas for the city's consideration and to discuss this pressing issue with East Boston residents.

Not only has FXB educated me on sustainability and advocacy, but it has also helped me move forward with drive and hope to make sustainable progress overpowering my fear of a future without change. I plan to double major in political science and environmental studies in college, in preparation for a career in environmental law. I hope that my work with FXB will only be the start of my advocacy journey, and that I can use my career to defend the health of vulnerable groups from climate change.

– by *Annika Johnson*

A Green Math

Skyscrapers and whale sharks. Apart from their monstrous size, some might not see any connection between these two items. But as a native New Yorker and an avid scuba diver, they both occupy a special place in my heart. Both, in their own way, led to my passion for climate advocacy.

It's hard to describe the feeling of being underwater with a whale shark. Swimming next to that gentle giant instilled in me a reverence for the majestic beauty and power of nature. I wanted to learn more about the species. What I found was a depressing picture of endangerment due to habitat destruction and overfishing.

What started with whale sharks then broadened to a curiosity about our oceans in general. I read worrisome tales of ocean acidification – a phenomenon I experienced first-hand when I returned to a reef I had previously visited, only to find a barren wasteland where there had once been vibrant wildlife and colourful coral.

The more I learned, the more concerned I felt about the way humanity mistreats this essential element of our planet. The ocean produces half the oxygen we breathe and absorbs fifty times more carbon dioxide than the atmosphere. I realized we don't need to protect the oceans to save only marine life. We need to protect it to save ourselves.

Living in New York City, it's easy to be removed from such concerns. It's a temple to the feats of human ingenuity, a bastion of modernity and technology that stands in stark contrast to the natural world. You don't necessarily feel the effects of climate change directly. At least not yet. But living there, I am acutely aware that the ethos of human progress born of the industrial age needs to be re-evaluated if we're going to continue to prosper. Yet, I am also aware of the potential for humans to radically alter the world in a matter of decades. New York fills me with trepidation at how much we need to change as a society and the inspiration that we will find a way to do so.

So, whale sharks and skyscrapers. I decided it was time to find a way to get involved. That's when I found FXB. My first couple of months as an FXB climate advocate were incredibly educational. The organization exposed me to scientific experts in the climate field, as well as politicians and everyday citizens that have been affected by our climate crisis. I gained the foundational knowledge needed to become an effective contributor, as well as became familiar with the more nuanced issues that add complexity to the conversation. I better understood the systemic issues surrounding climate change and the incentive structures that stand in the way of change.

It wasn't long before FXB empowered me to take on more responsibility. I was selected to interview Daphne Lundy, the Deputy Director of Social Resiliency at the Mayor's Office of New York City. Equipped with a set of questions and a healthy dose of impostor syndrome, I asked her about the mayor's plans to combat climate change, and how youth advocacy efforts can help complement them. It was an incredibly motivating experience to sit across from a public official and discuss tangible ways that I could affect change.

Six months into my time at FXB, another opportunity arose. The organization was putting together what they called a Liveable Cities Committee and invited me to be a member. As a born-and-raised city kid, the committee's mission, to find innovative ways to improve sustainability in urban areas, resonated deeply with me.

The three committee members met weekly with Karina L. Weinstein, Programme Strategy and Innovation Director, FXB USA, and Adrienne Dean, a member of the NYU Urban Health Lab and MPH candidate from the Icahn School of Medicine at Mount Sinai, who was helping mentor us. We discussed the most pressing climate issues in our city. Each student then chose a focus area and started to brainstorm ways to address them.

My focus area was mitigating carbon dioxide emissions. Trees absorb carbon dioxide, but not all trees are created equal in this endeavour. A bit of research pointed to the American sweetgum tree, in particular, as a particularly effective species, and one that is also native to the climate of the city. Propagating this kind of tree throughout the Bronx, the borough where I attend school, became my mission.

I calculated the total number of trees planted in the borough, as well as the percentage of these trees that were American sweetgums. The answer was very few. I then modelled the financial impact of these trees on the city, quantifying their environmental impact to frame them as an investment worth undertaking.

In the coming years, the Bronx plans to plant fifty thousand new trees, nearly doubling the number of trees the borough has at the moment. I hope that the research I've done will influence their selection of trees so that as many American sweetgums are planted as possible.

When I first considered getting involved in climate advocacy, it was hard to imagine myself having a meaningful impact. The crisis is so vast that it can feel overwhelming to take action. But FXB's guidance and resources have made me reconsider what's possible for youth advocates like myself. FXB helps students to break down this complex issue into smaller, more manageable pieces and set attainable incremental goals. I know that every ounce of carbon dioxide those sweetgum trees absorb is one less ounce destroying the coral reefs that I've been so lucky to experience. I hope the future generations will get an opportunity to experience them too. It is with this hope I continue my work with FXB. With their guidance and mentorship, I know I can grow into a leader in the fight against climate change.

– by *Jack Feinberg*

'FXB', FXB International (website). Last accessed on 27 March 2024. https://fxb.org/.

8

Climate Advocacy and Artificial Intelligence

Youth Advocacy – II

Karina Weinstein, Om Desai, Akash Pandya, Ansh Patel and Sid Desai

The AI Story

CLIMATE CHANGE IMPACTS PEOPLE OF ALL AGES, YET PRIMARILY only the young are the ones on the frontlines of addressing it. Even though these youngsters are not responsible for causing climate change, they will be the ones to experience its impact the most within their lifetimes. However, they have powerful technological tools and platforms to increase the effectiveness of their climate advocacy. Many youth utilize social-media platforms to amplify their messages and mobilize people around the globe. Not to forget, they have unprecedented access to information at a rapid pace.

Technological innovations enable them to access data that can be used to make a strong case for advocating for climate-change mitigation and adaptation.

Some of the publicly available data the youth utilizes include:

- NOAA Climate.gov is a source of timely and authoritative scientific data and information about climate. Its goals are to promote public understanding of climate science and climate-related events.
- Our World in Data provides research and data that can be used to make progress against the world's largest problems. There is data on CO_2 and greenhouse gas emissions.
- National Centers for Environmental Information is the leading authority for environmental data and manages one of the largest archives of atmospheric, coastal, geophysical and oceanic research in the world.
- SDGs Today features real-time and timely data on the Sustainable Development Goals (SDGs) and offers educational resources to support countries, institutions and civil society members to produce, share and engage with the data to help ensure that we meet the global goals by 2030.

FXB International provides opportunities for students to dive deeper into different topics such as the intersection between climate and health, sustainable consumption and energy. It also supports students' interests and skills, aiding them to use technology for social good, specifically to address climate action.

FXB USA approaches our work with youth climate leaders through two key frameworks: focusing on climate solutions and supporting students to select advocacy strategies that resonate with them. The focus on climate solutions promotes agency in our students. The world knows what needs to be done to address the climate crisis, but doing so is a matter of mobilizing people and necessary resources. The second aspect of our programme's strategy is that rather than dictating how students should get involved to address the climate crisis, we support students to chart their climate journeys and identify advocacy strategies that are aligned with their skills and interests.

When a cohort of nearly ten students with deep expertise in computer science and technology joined the FXB Climate Advocates programme, we immediately responded to their passion by creating the Artificial Intelligence (AI) & Climate Advocacy Committee. We believe it is critical to enable students to move away from being passive consumers of technology to becoming active change agents who use it to innovate and create. The students in this committee seek to harness AI and machine learning to accelerate progress on the climate crisis.

The vision of the AI & Climate Advocacy Committee is to build a platform consisting of ideas, knowledge, resources, mentors and support; to empower and inspire global young innovators, especially in remote parts of the world; and to create AI-enabled sustainable solutions to unique local issues related to building capacity and climate resilience. The students have proactively sought out seasoned AI professionals as mentors and attended numerous learning opportunities to enhance their knowledge. They are determined to inspire other youth to learn about how AI can be used to make a difference on climate change.

Through the incredible partnership with the Protect Our Planet Movement, the students in this committee have conducted numerous trainings and workshops for youth around the world on how to use free and available machine learning tools and data sets to address the climate crisis. The AI & Climate Advocacy Committee aspires to become a strong global team of influencers that can bring awareness among youth and adults about leveraging technology and innovation to achieve the SDG 13 on Climate Action.

The AI & Climate Advocacy Committee has outlined specific goals such as:

- Ideate concepts, proofs-of-concept and prototypes using available AI technologies for climate change mitigation and resilience.
- Advocate for the use of AI in climate advocacy through social media campaigns.
- Make AI more accessible to youth by providing opportunities to engage with available tools and techniques.

As someone who remembers when computers were first introduced, I am incredibly awed by how high school students are utilizing the technology to gain agency and create new initiatives to address the climate crisis. These young people are teaching adults around them to use new and emerging technologies and are demonstrating that they can lead on climate action, harnessing all of the tools at their disposal, including AI.

– by *Karina Weinstein*

Technology in Action

I spent much of my childhood wondering where the future would go. Would it be wondrous, or would it be horrible? The concept fascinated me, but at least to my knowledge at the age of seven, there was nothing I could do or that could happen that could really affect the future as a whole. Nevertheless, I felt that I should do whatever I could to leave my mark.

I had always enjoyed learning about science, and as I got older, I started reading with mounting worry about the threat of climate change. Initially, as I learned about the mechanisms behind climate change, I figured that this was a problem that I could simply leave to adults smarter than I was. But as I learned about the complexities that would keep us from being able to just suddenly stop climate change, I realized that this was a problem to be solved within my lifetime.

While all this was happening, I was experiencing the consequences of climate change. I'd always loved going out into parks and trails and looking at the wildlife, but I noticed that as the general climate of the area began to change, animals began to migrate away without returning the next year. Not only that, despite living in New Jersey that does not see much hurricane activity and has temperate weather, I noticed that as the years went by, there was a new costliest hurricane season ever recorded, and the area around my home was hit by multiple major hurricanes over my lifetime and more and more major storms every year.

I also learned that what I experienced growing up in a developed country paled in comparison to what climate change could do to poorer people in other parts of the world. When I went to India, I noticed that there was an increase in drought, with people struggling to put food on their tables due to the change in climate. Not only that, even in places with more modern amenities, the water was still not safe to drink due to chemicals leaking into the water from fertilizer and chemical contamination.

I noticed that although the effects of climate change did begin to hit affluent regions such as the United States or Europe, oftentimes some of the effects could be mitigated through programmes such as cooling, dams or alternative modes of importing food. However, India does not have these luxuries. This means that climate change would be utterly disastrous for much of the least developed world and affect billions of lives.

My desire to do something to protect the future was what led me into climate activism. The FXB Climate Advocates programme gave me a purpose to work towards and a way to affect real change in the world, using my knowledge and skills.

As I learned, read and experimented more, I became very interested in computer science and in making an algorithm that could address climate change. My friends and I found multiple areas where computer science could be very helpful in protecting the climate. Ansh Patel and I noticed that it was often hard for ordinary people to find a lot of climate data in one place. So, we created Dashboard.Earth, a platform that could combine climate data in an easy-to-see format, conveying the urgency of the problem and also acting like a monitor for the planet.

In another instance, Sid Desai and I created a programme that used both machine learning and image processing to detect deforestation from drone or satellite images, as well as combine the images with weather and resource data to automatically determine whether an area would be suitable for planting trees. This could provide massive support to reforestation and afforestation efforts, which often fail due to lack of knowledge about the proper area to place trees. On top of all of that, we recently received a grant from Microsoft AI for Earth to work on a machine learning system for camera traps that could automatically detect animals in areas different from where they usually are, which would help in monitoring animal populations and make tracking and restoring biodiversity much easier.

My climate journey was about realizing what a pressing issue climate change was, how many people were needed to solve it and knowing that I could use my passion for computer science to make a difference. I firmly believe that anybody can use their skills to help the fight against climate change, and everyone has their own story to tell about learning to fight for the future of the planet.

– by *Om Desai*

Assessing Patterns

Climate change is a topic that causes great debate regarding whether it is a real problem or not. It is perhaps difficult to fully comprehend the negative effects humans have on the environment until one personally sees it. If the world does not join together to combat this mounting crisis of rising sea levels and temperatures, we may not have the time to finish this debate altogether.

Around four years ago, my family and I went to India. Although the country has a rich cultural heritage, it unfortunately also has very poor air quality due in part to the amount of fossil fuels being emitted into the atmosphere. From the minute I walked out of Ahmedabad Airport, I could smell a stench in the air that irritated my nostrils. Furthermore, my vision was obscured at times due to the high concentration of dust in the air. For me, just staying outside for a couple of hours could result in an itchy throat or burning eyes. I was astonished to see that the homeless were forced to breathe this air constantly. At the time, I didn't fully understand that simply breathing would damage the residents' health. Throughout the trip, I observed the negative effects of climate change on the environment, particularly on those not fortunate enough to afford the means to combat it where they live.

As my family and I flew to the Caribbean Island of Antigua in 2018, we were all excited to relax on the beach and enjoy a week off before school started. However, once at the resort, we were informed of issues with high amounts of sargassum seaweed that had overtaken the shore making it difficult to enjoy the waters on the beach. My whole family and I were upset by the fact that the beaches were largely unapproachable due to the seaweed issue, but we would only later learn that many other coastal areas apart from Antigua are facing it. We observed a similar issue on a recent trip to Florida. I thought that there must be ways to better track when these patterns of seaweed could arrive at which coastal region via artificial intelligence. By leveraging these patterns, there may be a possibility to predict potential locations of high accumulation, and also prevent it from negatively impacting the vital tourism industries in these areas.

When I heard about FXB Climate Advocates, I was eager to join because it fights for a cause that I believe in. I believe that it is everyone's responsibility to aid in bettering the climate in whatever way they can, no matter the scale of what they do.

– by *Akash Pandya*

'Dashboard.Earth'

The motivating factor for me to join the FXB Climate Advocates programme was to educate myself and others on the negative consequences of climate change. The anthropogenic release of greenhouse gases into the atmosphere is causing global warming. The results of such warming are destructive and life endangering. The lives of millions of people living in coastal cities are in danger. Global warming will lead to rising sea levels, cities will be submerged, and people will be left homeless. Humans won't be the only species affected by global warming; many endangered species will go extinct, and entire ecosystems will collapse.

The AI & Climate Advocacy Community provided me the opportunity to work with like-minded peers on projects such as 'Dashboard.Earth'. This interactive dashboard is a dynamic tool that can be used to view the health of the atmosphere, biomes, oceans and other crucial factors that enable life on Earth. The platform provides a quick means to educate people about the severity of climate change and help identify where to start taking action. I hope to continue to contribute to this project so that climate change doesn't go unnoticed.

– by *Ansh Patel*

Reconciling With The Ground-Reality

I've been very curious and inquisitive ever since I could talk. Imagine a four-year-old kid, stumbling around, pointing at everything and anything, blabbering, 'Mom what is that?', 'Dad, what is that?' This early obsession sparked my passion to read and learn. I began to keep myself occupied by learning basic programming and technology skills. Soon, I progressed from basic block coding such as Scratch and began to explore the world of AI and machine learning.

While reading the news, I came across an article by *National Geographic*, 'Why Cape Town Is Running Out of Water, and Who's Next'. It immediately caught my eye. I wondered, how can humans run out of something as bountiful and basic as water? This was my first insight into the repercussions of climate change on the real world. Climate change has the ability to deprive people in some parts of the world of a basic resource such as water!

I began to dive deeper into the effects of climate change and learned the magnitude of its impact on people across the world. People all over the world were struggling for basic needs such as food, water and shelter due to climate change. Newly inspired to make change, I began looking for ways to use my skills and interests in AI and technology to benefit the movement against climate change.

This was when I was introduced to FXB Climate Advocates' AI & Climate Advocacy Committee. Through this committee I was able to work with young and like-minded peers to fight towards a common goal using the latest technology available. We have been exploring a potential solution for climate change which was both very new and relatively uncharted. Over the last year and a half as a part of this amazing collaboration, we have been able to make a real difference to a very imminent problem.

– by *Sid Desai*

'Founder & History', FXB International (website). Last accessed on 27 March 2024. https://fxb.org/who-we-are/founder-history/.

Craig Welch, 'Why Cape Town Is Running Out of Water, and Who's Next', *National Geographic*, 06 March 2018. Last accessed on 27 March 2024. https://www.nationalgeographic.com/science/article/cape-town-running-out-of-water-drought-taps-shutoff-other-cities#:~:text=Population%20growth%20and%20a%20record,July%2C%20when%20the%20city%20says.

9

A Climate Crusader's Vision

Youth Advocacy – III

Ash Pachauri, Philo Magdalene A, Erik Solheim and Shailly Kedia

'While climate change is an existential threat to humanity, it's also an enormous opportunity. Investments in solar and wind energy, in electric mobility and green cities, in tree planting and conservation not only benefit Mother Earth, they also provide jobs and prosperity. That's why we see developing nations like India and China investing more and more in green business. It's a win-win opportunity. For the first time in human history policies and investment opportunities are available which create wealth, improve livelihoods and secure the environment at the same time.

– Dr Erik Solheim, Former Executive Director, United Nations Environment Programme and Patron, World Sustainable Development Forum

The Challenge

FROM IMPERIALISM AND WORLD WARS TO PLAGUES AND pandemics, anthropogenic conflicts and challenges have been an essential condition of human civilization throughout history. In confronting them, humanity has invariably managed to move on with resilience and perseverance, albeit with great losses. This intense familiarity of dealing with endless adversities, however, does little to sensitize us to the historically unparalleled crusade of the 21st century: climate change and environmental degradation.

'Warming of the climate system is unequivocal, and since the 1950s, many of the observed changes are unprecedented over decades to millennia. The atmosphere and ocean have warmed, the amounts of snow and ice have diminished, sea level has risen, and the concentrations of greenhouse gases have increased.' This was the conclusion arrived in the Fifth Assessment Report (AR5) of the Intergovernmental Panel on Climate Change (IPCC), that assessed over 30,000 scientific papers involving over 830 scientists as lead authors, over 1,000 contributing authors and over 1,000 expert reviewers.

The report clearly established that the atmospheric concentrations of carbon dioxide, methane and nitrous oxide have been unprecedented in at least the last 8,00,000 years. The consequential warming of the climate system has also been unequivocal and has had widespread impacts on human and natural systems on all continents and across the oceans. Impacts are due to observed climate change, irrespective of its cause, indicating the sensitivity of natural and human systems to changing climate. Changes in many extreme weather and climate events have been observed since about 1950. Some of these changes have been linked to human influences, including a decrease in cold temperature extremes, an increase in warm temperature extremes, an increase in extreme high sea levels and an increase in the number of heavy precipitation events in a number of regions.

It is very likely that heat waves will occur more often and last longer, and that extreme precipitation events will become more intense and frequent in many regions. The ocean will continue to warm and acidify, while global mean sea level will rise. Climate change will amplify existing risks and create new risks for natural and human systems. Risks are unevenly distributed and are generally greater for disadvantaged people and communities in countries at all levels of development.

The 21st century has seen the world acknowledge that anthropocentric growth and development that occurred since the advent of Industrial Revolution has numbed the very psyche of humanity against one's inherent responsibility to nature. As the modern development paradigm augmented by human attitudes and behaviours have staggering implications on the environment, it is incumbent that in addition to the role of governments and businesses, we foster large-scale community participation, each in their own localized manner, to create a groundswell movement that centralizes environmental discourse and social consciousness. Propelling this new trajectory of thought and action requires concerted, yet diversified effort which can be made possible by the championing of youth leadership.

The POP Movement

Dr R.K. Pachauri, former Chairman (2002–15) of the IPCC conceptualized a programme, which he named POP (Protect Our Planet) Movement to involve youth in efforts to address climate change. He believed the youth of the world represented hope and offered an alternative to business as usual. 'There is an urgent need for a very different global approach for dealing with the climate change challenge,' he said.

While serving as the chairman of the IPCC, Dr Pachauri noted that young people had begun approaching world leaders to express their disillusionment and frustration at the fact that not enough was being done to protect the future of the younger generations. Dr Pachauri came to the conclusion that it is the youth of the world who have to take the lead in finding and implementing solutions to protect our planet from disasters resulting from human actions and in convincing policymakers to take effective measures to urgently address this issue. It was with this vision, that Dr Pachauri established the POP Movement in 2016 on the occasion of Earth Day. The POP Movement functions on the belief that youth leading climate actions on the ground is the ideal way for building and propagating a sustained environmental movement that is inclusive of all stakeholders in society.

The movement goes beyond the scope of advocacy or public demonstration of dissent against governments, businesses and lawmakers, and aims at mobilizing youth-led community efforts to address environmental degradation through implementing innovative solutions and adopting sustainable lifestyles.

Figure 1: Various levels of youth influence for climate action

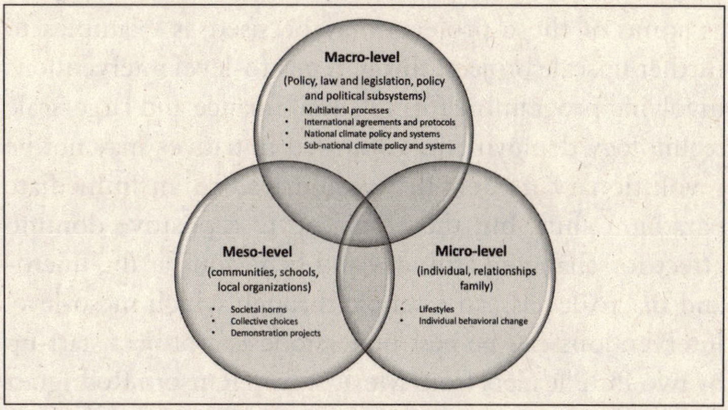

Source: Compiled by authors

For too long, youth-led climate change movements and initiatives have focused much of their efforts on interventions at the macro- and micro-level. Meso-level interventions at the organizational and local community-level are also much needed as they offer potential to act as a bridge between the macro- and micro-levels. Meso-level interventions can be driven by policy change (top down) as well as through grassroots initiative (ground up).

At the time the POP Movement was conceptualized, it was felt that there is a need for a stronger bridge between the macro-level and meso-level and also between the meso-level and micro-level. Meso-level interventions involve not only raising awareness through advocacy and strikes to influence actions at the macro- and micro-levels but also to proactively demonstrate concrete examples of actions which could help individual as well as collective action. Demonstration projects at the meso-level are also important as some of these projects may be used as examples to further upscale projects through macro-level interventions involving programme formulation, finance and large-scale technology deployment. Youth-led initiatives may not be revolutionary models that would lead to an immediate paradigm shift, but they can lead to a positive domino effect for changing attitudes and behaviour at the micro- and macro-levels. An example through which meso-level interventions can be best understood is a project start-up by two POP leaders from Mexico, Iván Ransom Rodríguez and Kevin Morales Münstermann. Conceived in Academia Borussia in Mexico and supported by the German soccer team Borussia Dortmund, their project 'Resilience 2020' seeks to build resilience in households, businesses and farmers through free-of-cost implementation of eco-technologies and a local circular economy model. Aligning with each of the seventeen sustainable development goals, the project promotes sustainable eco-technologies that improves people's affordability.

Grassroots initiatives such as these not only promote the efficient use of resources and transform the way individuals produce and consume, but these macro-level interventions can be upscaled for large-scale impact toward sustainability. This has been affirmed by the duo during a capacity building session organized by the POP Movement when they noted, 'We are truly convinced that the project has a promising future, for it is a simple and yet powerful idea taken into action. It will provide people with some of their basic needs (water, food, electricity and gas) and generate savings and an extra income. Moreover, its innovative core and replicability contributes to its exponential growth potential.'

Another similar example is that of a youth-led and community-centred climate group 'Fersaamb' founded by two POP leaders, Fernando Castro Bojórquez and Saúl Ernesto López. Specialists in environmental engineering, the pair works to empower their neighbourhood by sharing knowledge on civil-society protection and providing environmental services. They engage with communities through door-to-door interactions where consensus is built on the need to operationalize environmental consciousness in their suburban neighbourhood and activities that stimulate behavioural and lifestyle changes among residents. The team also coordinates with the local municipality and administration to implement civil-protection plans.

To the common eye, Fernando and Saúl may come across as ordinary young graduates, but they are hailed as real-life heroes by the POP family they are a part of. They encounter all the challenges of a young person in struggling to overcome logistical difficulties, manage part-time jobs to support themselves and their environmental work and balance other priorities. Their vision and resolve driving them forward is strengthened by their many support systems, which include the POP Movement. The movement helps them find new arenas to share their work and draw learnings and inspirations from the diverse people they meet. Some platforms that they have engaged in the past include the International Conference and POP Festival for Youth-led Climate Action in Mexico, 17th World Summit of Nobel Peace Laureates in Mérida and the Second World Sustainable Development Forum in Durango, Mexico. The continued support and mentorship they receive through the POP Movement is complemented by the fact that they are also connected with environmental enthusiasts across the globe as a part of the POP global community. Consisting of individuals representing various fields from different sectors and sections of society, this close-knit community of POP exchange their experiences and milestones, form collaborations, support and mentor each other and more importantly, move with collective solidarity.

Meso-level initiatives such as the ones discussed above are not exclusively youth-centric processes but involve the active support and engagement of multiple stakeholders including academic and research communities, local residentiaries, governments and businesses.

The POP Movement was launched with the aim of mobilizing the youth of the world to take the lead in promoting sustainable development and contribute to mitigating the emissions of Greenhouse Gases (GHGs) and adapting to the impacts of climate change, which are now inevitable, given the concentration of GHGs in the past. To mobilize the 1.8 billion youth between the ages of 10 and 24 years, they would need to be informed about the consequences of inaction, which would adversely affect their future, and the attractiveness of action, which would reduce the risks they are projected to face and create a cleaner, sustainable world for them to live in. In the age of social consciousness where youth live in, grow amidst and draw from socially and politically charged environments, the social involvement of young people that goes beyond self-interest has been increasingly normalized. This inspirational and resourceful power of politically and socially informed young people in the movement of climate action offers the highest optimism.

Youth Inspired by Knowledge

Since its launch in 2016, the POP Movement has grown from a concept to a global phenomenon. There are hundreds of institutions globally striving towards solutions as a part of the POP Movement. The organization now working with over 1.2 million youth, in 55-plus countries with over 300 partners.

The key change that the POP Movement seeks to create is a community with commitment across the globe that is fully conscious of the future that lies ahead given today's inertia. Youth, with increasing environmental and sociopolitical consciousness, are therefore, willing to take a lead not only to create a new culture in their community and educational institutions, but also exert pressure upwards on policy-makers and administrators. The POP Movement nurtures such a movement of 'youth inspired by knowledge' for scaling up and creating a community of climate-responsive young people across the globe.

Resting on a fundamental nexus between local interventions and global symbiosis, the organization's efforts can be grouped under, but are not limited to, four main umbrellas: Capacity building, knowledge sharing, advocacy and implementation. Having conducted over 550 awareness-building activities, advocacy sessions and training workshops till date, the POP Movement not only builds capacities of youth for sustainable action, but also serves as an interactive and knowledge space to mobilize individual and collective action among youth and other stakeholders in implementing solutions needed to mitigate and adapt to climate change. It is noteworthy that most of the POP youth from different parts of the world who are now leaders in advocacy and action, were once motivated individuals who had come forward in these inclusive spaces created by the movement with expressive intent to lead innovation and/or community action.

Empowering youth and trusting them to lead has come to be viewed as the ideal road ahead as the world ventures to evolve a new narrative of development which is sensitive to protecting the global commons and the earth's ecosystems. It is high time that public and private institutions including civil society emerge from their conservative attitudes of trust, allowing young minds to take the lead and help orchestrate the way forward. It is this very foundational concept that POP Movement endorses as it guides youth to be leaders and mentors themselves. POP Global Youth Mentor, Vanessa Hernández is one among the many individuals who exemplifies this mission. A student of pharmaceutical chemistry and biology, she established an active POP community in her university in 2018 having been introduced to the movement through a conference in the same year and went on to undertake multifarious roles in the POP Movement including outreach, peer motivation and programme coordination for youth around the world. With unending enthusiasm, Vanessa supports the implementation of projects conceived by the POP community in her university, and furthermore, guides and motivates students, specifically those across Latin America to foster environmental consciousness and develop specific projects. She enjoys everything she does and every experience she has with the POP Movement, which she believes, has significantly contributed to her personal and professional growth. Her all-encompassing leadership stands as one of the integral forces behind the success of various POP initiatives including the International Conference and POP Festival for Youth-led Climate Action in 2019.

Mentorship and Networking for Climate Action Now

Members of the POP family strive towards taking concrete actions for addressing climate change through youth-led initiatives and strong steps. There are ample examples in this regard. The 'Julius-Stursberg-Gymnasium' school of Germany is one such example which strives to build environmental consciousness amongst its students. Unlike the mainstream sustainability groups found in many schools that often focus on awareness campaigns alone, POP Germany stands out for collaborating with the school management and city council in the implementation of contemporary ideas and sustainable solutions on campus. A successful example of an initiative by a POP Family member is Project Nishtha (Project Faith) where Suhanee Giroti, a high school student, developed a corporate social-responsibility project with the Angelique International Limited, and installed a composting machine at a temple in New Delhi for waste recycling. Temple flowers were processed for composting and the manure was used in gardens around the temples, creating a circular flow of resources. The POP Movement along with the World Sustainable Development Forum (WSDF) seeks to encourage and document such youth initiatives so that youth are not merely seen as protestors with placards on the streets but also as demonstrators of solutions and leaders of change.

World Sustainable Development Forum: An Intergenerational Forum

The World Sustainable Development Forum (WSDF) was set up in tandem with the POP Movement, seeded from Dr Pachauri's disillusionment with global economic forums where large section of the business community and other stakeholders continued to neglect critical environmental problems facing humanity. WSDF was founded to overcome this and bridge the gap between political leaders from different levels, and leaders of business, research and academia and civil society from different corners of the world to share knowledge and experiences about the latest developments on policies, technologies and programmes and create resolve for action at the grassroots level by all stakeholders.

Politicians, scientists, academics, civil society and business leaders, artists, youth and others are responsible for taking deliberate actions related to the multi-stakeholder implementation of the Paris Agreement and the Sustainable Development Goals. The WSDF's actions are well synergized with POP Movement. The POP brings the youth momentum to nudge macro-level leadership and ambition by bringing voices and impacts from interventions at the meso-level and micro-level. Meanwhile, the WSDF serves as a multi-generational platform, which enables these stakeholders to discuss important issues of sustainable development but more importantly to initiate actions to address the growing challenge of climate change. Recognizing the complementarity of WSDF and the POP Movement, it is clear that the two should interact to synergize their impact.

A key area of synergy would be needed to start with a dialogue across generations. In most high-level international events including those by intergovernmental organizations, the voice of youth is merely engaged in the form of 'tokenism' wherein they briefly address a large gathering mostly consisting of adults. A gap has been seen in truly involving young people in terms of inter-generational dialogue. The WSDF attempts to bridge that gap by serving as a platform that is inclusive of youth from different strata in the most realistic sense. Thus, when WSDF convened in Mexico in 2018, the youth from the POP Movement were involved as active participants. And in 2020, when WSDF met again in Mexico, 1,200 young people from 27 countries joined forming one-third of the audience.

Each of the ten plenary sessions at WSDF 2020 engaged youth together with heads of states and global decision makers. The youth present led the forum's flagship session, which Dr Pachauri named as 'Youthquake and the POP Movement', and young people discussed the importance of amplifying their voices and meaningfully engaging in framing policy and programmes to protect our planet in it. The role of young people in the discussions at this platform inspired the members of WSDF to move their agenda forward. In turn, youth from the POP Movement were inspired to strengthen their advocacy and action and undertake more projects with determination and collective vigour, which were meaningful in their respective countries to promote sustainable lifestyles and climate action. Since their inception, the WSDF and the POP Movement have been further invigorated to pursue a common agenda. In addition to organizing global and regional WSDF meetings, the two organizations work together, often connecting the patrons and members of WSDF with the youth of POP to not only deliberate on, but also to implement actions to realize the WSDF's declarations.

The Climate Crusader's Vision Lives On

The COVID-19 crisis, like a mirror, reflected the great value, foresight, and clear warnings of the IPCC's Fourth and Fifth Assessment Reports, which were released during Dr Pachauri's chairmanship. As a result of the pandemic, a new sense of urgency has been felt to reverse the path the world has taken and define a new sustainable future, which protects our planet and the species that inhabit it.

'A people's movement is essential for such a reversal in a very short period of time. It is for the youth of the world to take the lead and ensure that the economic, technological and managerial strength of modern society is harnessed effectively to move quickly in the right direction. We need to keep in mind Gandhi's advice that, speed is irrelevant if you are going in the wrong direction,' Dr

Pachauri has stated. The programmes that Dr Pachauri's organizations are undertaking will undoubtedly set us in the right direction and continue his crusade as their efforts multiply, grow and develop over the coming years. This may be viewed as a befitting legacy for Dr Pachauri and his lifetime work as a climate crusader.

'Fifth Assessment Report', IPCC (website). Last accessed on 27 March 2024. https://www.ipcc.ch/assessment-report/ar5/.

'Home', World Sustainable Development Forum (website). Last accessed on 27 March 2024. https://worldsdf.org/.

'Observed Changes and their Causes', IPCC (website). Last accessed on 27 March 2024. https://ar5-syr.ipcc.ch/topic_observedchanges.php#:~:text=Observed%20changes%20in%20the%20climate,and%20sea%20level%20has%20risen.

Philo Magdalene, 'Community engagement in the face of environmental crisis – Where the real work begins', POP Movement (website), January 2020. Last accessed on 27 March 2024. https://thepopmovement.org/pop_stories/community-engagement-in-the-face-of-environmental-crisis-where-the-real-work-begins/.

10

Inspired by Knowledge

Youth Advocacy – IV

Ash Pachauri, Norma P. Muñoz Sevilla,
Vanessa Anahí Hernández Vázquez,
Drishya Pathak, Komal Mittal,
Ana Hanhausen Doménech, H.E. Rosalía Arteaga
and Philo Magdalene A

> 'It is for the youth of the world to take the lead and ensure that the economic, technological and managerial strength of modern society is harnessed effectively to move quickly in the right direction. We need to keep in mind Gandhi's advice that speed is irrelevant if you are going in the wrong direction. A people's movement is essential for such a reversal in a very short period of time.'
>
> – *Dr R.K. Pachauri*

SINCE THE INCEPTION OF THE PROTECT OUR PLANET (POP) Movement, the vision has been to foster an atmosphere that engages youngsters around the globe in an imaginative, inventive and participatory way to promote leadership that is led by actions and solutions towards environmental conservation and sustainable development. In a continuous quest to create dynamic and inclusive spaces that manufacture conviction and motivate young innovators and changemakers, the POP Movement has endeavoured to design several youth-led and youth-centred initiatives that are also intergenerational and multi-stakeholder. This chapter presents three initiatives of the POP Movement to demonstrate that youth inspired by knowledge and mentored by values will build a movement that the world needs today to protect the planet. Two out of three of these initiatives were launched during the COVID-19 pandemic.

The lockdown pushed us into a world of remote work and has been a crucial global challenge in the continuation climate action activities. While this is no doubt a constraint, virtual environments do offer opportunities to improvise work formats and connect us more than ever before. The POP Movement tapped into the benefits of technology and the ever greater need to heighten consciousness about the impact of human-induced action on the health and survival of the planet and its species. Its interventions have paved the way for international collaboration among and between young environmental advocates that was not thought to be possible before. This opportunity was enhanced through the POP Movement's initiatives – the POP Festival, the Latin America Dialogue and the POP Conclave – which have all led to partnerships and alliances between young participants from different sectors, communities and geographies.

The POP Festival: Our Annual Flagship Event

The POP Festival, a youth-inspired platform to share, learn and empower, is unique and stands out. The POP Movement's annual flagship event was envisioned to bring together young people from different parts of the world to celebrate and share hope, connect with each other and develop a sense of solidarity towards addressing the climate crisis. This venture came about not only to encourage youth leadership on climate action, but also to serve as an opportunity to develop and widen the reach of youth-led intervention models through the presence of multiple stakeholders. Moving away from institutionalized standards and strict protocols that often deter the creative ideation and optimal engagement of young people in forums, this event embraces the ideas and projects of youth, encourages them to take initiative and provides them a platform to showcase and enrich their work in both local and global contexts. Unlike many clichéd conferences, this platform nurtures hope and a feeling of celebration – a sustained festive element and a sense of exuberance accompanies the presentation of youth-led projects and initiatives through creative approaches, fostering a sense of togetherness.

In its debut event in 2019, the POP Festival witnessed over ten presentations, six workshops, and seven exhibits and posters, a music concert and a stage play – all making a concordance of creative elements with each synchronized towards a common theme of climate action. Multiple formats such as these which have since been used at each edition, each more diversified based on specific contexts, not only serve as effective knowledge exchange tools, but also exemplify the creative and celebratory spirit of the POP Festival. Projects and initiatives are rewarded on the basis of various criteria that include effectiveness of the business model, promotion of sustainable development, environmental protection, support and innovation, and civil society engagement. Furthermore, prizes are given to projects that display exceptional leadership by the coordinators.

In addition to active youth involvement, the POP Festival thrives from partnerships with various stakeholders including governments, businesses, academia and civil society. In alignment with its strong principles of inclusion and amplifying voices, the POP Festival also embraces the active engagement of indigenous communities from Latin America and around the world.

The POP Festival empowers youth, ideas and communities, serving as a space for self-expression, cross-learning and collaboration. Moving beyond networking and knowledge sharing, what the POP Festival largely aims at is to strengthen the resolve of communities, build capacities and instil values that foster social responsibility, environmental consciousness, and inspiration to work towards reducing greenhouse gas emissions among other objectives to protect the planet.

Latin America Dialogue

Since its launch in Mexico in 2016, the POP Movement has been very active in the Latin America region. With its unwavering belief in the potential of youth and the power of collectivization, the POP Movement very deliberately acts to support youth and communities in Latin America in order to generate change for a better future. Latin America, similar to the rest of the planet, faces the threatening impacts of climate change. Thus, it was thought important for the region to come together to take concerted action through open dialogue that inspires the commitment of youth and other stakeholders. It is with this idea that the Latin America Dialogue was launched.

The first Latin America Dialogue was organized on 22 April 2020, which marked fifty years of Earth Day, in partnership with Her Excellency Dr Rosalía Arteaga, a global leader and strong proponent of climate leadership and education. Held virtually due to the lockdown, the initiative brought together young people leading grassroots projects in dialogue with Her Excellency to discuss initiatives that can be implemented to advance climate action.

The Latin America Dialogue is not merely a platform for the voice of Latin American youth. Rather, it underscores the collective power of bringing together the perspectives of different sectors and stakeholders. These sectors include government, academia, legislation, media, civil society, science and technology, and indigenous communities to name a few. Through the Dialogue, these stakeholders come together to deliberate about cross-sectoral, community-oriented and youth-led efforts for climate action and sustainable development within the sphere of the Latin American region.

Values-driven Approach to Dialogue

In allegiance to its strong values of participatory dialogue and inclusion, the Latin America Dialogue engages youth, community and stakeholders in ongoing two-way discussions in order to recognize and address issues, challenges and questions that are of relevance and significance to the community itself. Thus, rather than unilaterally deciding on themes of focus for the Latin America Dialogue, the POP Movement adopts a multi-stakeholder perspective in which it listens to communities and understands their needs and challenges to arrive at themes for deliberation. This approach is equitable and inclusive and allows integrity in the selection of topics of relevance to explore during the Latin America Dialogue.

Prior to the second edition of Latin America Dialogue, which was held on 22 July 2020, an interactive workshop was conducted to understand the most pressing environmental problems in the Latin America region. This workshop gathered perspectives of different communities from multiple sectors including youth, social, indigenous, academia, media, legislative and NGOs from different countries such as Ecuador, Mexico, Colombia, Chile, Paraguay, Bolivia, El Salvador and Venezuela, in order to explore environmental challenges and solutions.

The outcomes of the discussion from the perspective of highly varied sectors were astonishingly similar. They discussed issues and concerns, which included invasion of territories; illegal logging; deforestation; mass commercialization of agricultural land; land use changes; wide use of pesticides resulting in pollution, contamination, toxicity, and health impacts; exploitation of aquifers; changes in water quality; exploitation of resources by mining and extractive industries; mining concessions; loss of ancient, indigenous wisdom, culture, and language; and human rights violations to name a few.

The second event brought together stakeholders in large numbers, including those from the interactive workshop, to engage with and seek solutions to the problems flagged during the pre-dialogue meeting. It was a gratifying experience for the participants to be exposed to a multitude of perspectives of diverse communities. Keynote speaker Her Excellency Dr Rosalía Arteaga shared her insights and inspiration. She said:

'I must point out that the wealth of the workshop organized with the participation of various sectors of society is an example of inclusion and of what we must do day-by-day. Academia and the scientific community must socialize in order to produce the necessary knowledge and transform it; NGOs play a very important role and together with the media they can create adequate coverage of issues relevant to all populations. Indigenous communities contribute to regional knowledge and issues and the social and legislative sectors combine to consolidate the foundations of community development.'

Ms Camila González, a 16-year-old activist, highlighted that many young people are looking for opportunities to get involved and they need to be allowed in important spaces and 'be seen as part of the solution'. Balmore Zanco, a 32-year-old representative of the indigenous community from the Nahua Pipil community, El Salvador, stated that in order to protect biodiversity and marine-coastal resources in Latin America, strengthened alliances among indigenous communities, policy making and governments are a must. He emphasized that indigenous community members are commonly hailed as 'guardians of nature' that protect natural territories against invasion and degradation.

The two Latin America Dialogues held so far have witnessed the exchange of perspectives and ideas, collaboration and commitment that inspire and motivate the youth to engage in action on multiple fronts. This overarching vision also involves building a sense of solidarity among stakeholders and exchanging ideas for cross-learning and networking that could be undertaken beyond the Dialogue.

Inception of the POP Conclave

With a deep appreciation for mobilizing determined efforts across extensive spheres to overcome the ecological challenges caused by the Anthropocene, the POP Movement set out in search of an innovative communication strategy that would enable a strong sense of unity and purpose during the COVID-19 pandemic. When countries locked down to contain the pandemic, members of the POP family from different parts of the world looked for a way to interact. This led to the inception of weekly virtual conversations with young leaders from every continent including Asia, Africa, Australia, Europe and the Americas.

During the weekly intra-continental calls that took place, many of the POP youth expressed interest in furthering the network and enhancing partnerships through cross-continent conversations. As systematic response to this interest, the POP Conclave project was conceived, aiming to expand the network of young social leaders by connecting them with their peers from across continents and creating an opportunity to cross-learn in the process of sharing insights, context-based experience and helping each other build individual and collective strategies for grassroots action. The factors that were crucial in planning the POP Conclave were balancing sometimes very varied time zones across continents, merging a wide range of youth interests, facilitating appropriate mentorship and guidance throughout the process, and ensuring equal distribution of participants among groups with diverse geographies, knowledge and experience. The conclave allows youth from around the world to interact and share ideas and actions through virtual meetings, where conversations focus on addressing environmental concerns and supporting collaboration through sharing climate action and initiatives on sustainable development.

'Home', The POP Movement (website), Last accessed on 27 March 2024. https://thepopmovement.org/.

11

Co-existence

A Possibility

Dhawan Rawat

I WAS A TOURIST WHO LOVED GOING TO THE MOUNTAINS. BUT I never realized the impact of my visits or the conflicts at play in these regions.

It was my trips to these terrains that enticed me into joining the Indian Forest Service, and it was during my preparation for the Union Public Service Commission (UPSC) exam, and after having joined the service, that I understood the significance of the forests and their role in human existence.

During our field visits while training, I came across scenarios where human impact was destroying the forests, rivers and wildlife. Meanwhile, there were also scenarios where human will was restoring the affected ecosystem. This changed my thinking process and outlook. I had already joined the service, and my major goal since then has been to make people a part of the conservation efforts. It is only when the communities closest to these forests come together that the damage can be undone.

Now, the Question Is How?

The human side of conservation can never be sidelined as humans have the biggest impact on the environment. In a few years of being in the forest service, I have realized that the things that seem logical and common knowledge to many such as forests being the source of rivers, wildlife helping in the regeneration of forests etc., are not so well-known among the masses. The communities living close to these forests are among the poorest. For them, the forest is a major economic resource more than anything else. Awareness does sensitize these populations, but the economic part of the problem cannot be neglected. This is where government policy and its implementation plays a significant role. Providing alternative sources of income and making these communities stakeholders in the process of conservation can have a lasting impact. Involvement of local communities and making them in charge of the growth of eco-tourism around protected areas has been successful in several instances. These successful models need to be implemented across the country with regional modifications. Everyone wants something to come out of their efforts. If there is a suitable incentive for these communities, they can surely become the protectors of forest and wildlife, and the biggest opponents of unwanted encroachment in the name of development.

Today, environmental changes are visible and are affecting a large part of the population across the globe. Climate unpredictability is increasing like never before, and yet, we still prefer to ignore it because we believe it has not arrived at our doorstep. This attitude needs to change. We should not forget that no matter what we do, we are part of this ecosystem which can only sustain itself as long as we maintain a balance. Environmental consciousness needs to become a part of every government policy and deliberation. It should be an addition to Gandhi's Talisman.

Development vs. Conservation

This is an age-old debate – whether a developing country such as India should focus on forest conservation. For many spear holders of development, Forest Acts are a hurdle and need to be amended. The moment I say development, the images that come to our mind are big buildings, highways, malls, etc. We have been conditioned to see these as symbols of development. These components are surely important, but development is not merely defined by these indicators. The priority of development initiatives should be to invest in basic healthcare, education and waste management. The most important component is fast delivery of citizen services. What is the point of developing a few cities when the common man has to run here and there for basic services.

I will explain this through the example of Finland. During our visit to Finland, we learnt that 13 per cent of the country's economy is bio-economy. Almost every citizen is dependent on the forests, and most of these forests are privately owned. Forest-based industries are well developed and even electricity is generated by pyrolization of wood waste. Forests are managed scientifically. The cities surely have big infrastructure, but the rural part, which is more than 95 per cent of the country, is also well-connected to citizen services. In these parts, there are no big buildings, but they have world-class public transport connectivity, internet, local markets, electricity, one-point government delivery of services, best in the world schools, and hospitals to cater to the needs of every citizen living in these villages. The forests play such a big role in every citizen's life that life without them is unimaginable. This reflects living in harmony with the environment in the truest sense. This is the kind of development we need, not just jungles of concrete.

A Story of Change from the Field

The area around Mouling National Park in Arunachal Pradesh is inhabited by the Adi tribe. When I joined as Divisional Forest Officer (DFO) here, I found that they have had an annual hunting festival that has been held from time immemorial. Though the festival is surely a part of their culture, it has become unsustainable as the old bows and arrows have been replaced by sophisticated air guns. I didn't want this mass hunting event to take place, but it was not easy. I knew that the mere implementation of law won't change things for long. We needed to change the mindset first. We started an awareness campaign to inform the locals about the potential the site held for eco-tourism and the benefits it could have for the community. We also appealed to them to stop using guns, as they weren't a part of the tradition and their use was wrong in every sense. The campaign helped, but I knew that we needed something weightier to make them understand. We started asking the younger generation how many species of birds they had seen around their villages. Was it the same that their forefathers' had seen? Here, we touched a nerve. We emphasized that if the mass hunting continued, the next generations would only get to see the wildlife in picture books or as plastic models.

The result was unbelievable – village and youth organizations promised not to hunt, and they kept their promise. Within a year, I was able to record around 100 species around town – these had not been present before. This is a small change, but it will lead to bigger results. It was all possible because of community participation.

The Future

Environment conservation is not a lost cause; there is still time if we all work together. There are hundreds of success stories in which ordinary people have come together for the sake of the environment. We need to mobilize the younger generation who will grow into responsible citizens. Environmental themes should become a core part of our education system.

That said, conservation does not have to take an isolated approach; it should be a part of our development process. India has always been an example to the world when it comes to people living in harmony with nature. Our culture respects every living being and entity which sustain life on the planet. Coexistence is possible if we provide space to nature and do not take over the land because of our greed.

I am a firm believer of animal ethics, which means wild animals have an equal right to live on this planet. Conflicts arise when we leave nothing for these animals. We would act much like them if someone encroaches on our space.

The way ahead lies in recognizing the role every living being plays in maintaining the ecosystem. We have to increase green spaces in both urban and rural areas. The mangroves and riverine ecosystems need to be restored to minimize the impact of cyclones, tsunamis and floods. Waste currently is, and in the coming days will remain, one of the biggest problems for our country. We need to invest in efficient waste-disposal mechanisms. Indians have always been good at recycling. This tendency needs to be promoted and appreciated, rather than promoting Western consumerist attitude of 'use and throw'.

Whenever I address a gathering I always say, 'Everyone wants to rush to the forest for their leisure time, but nobody wants to save it'. During weekends and holidays, the rush we see in hill stations and national parks is proof that more and more people want to experience the purity of nature. These people also need to be sensitized to become responsible tourists. They need to become responsible for their acts, while they are visiting forests and after they come back.

Every person who admires the beauty of nature needs to understand that these rivers and forests which are jewels of this planet are under extreme pressure and need help from everyone. When citizens become aware, the system will surely recognize development as a progressive move in harmony with nature.

Then, the coexistence of conservation and development, people and wildlife, forests and roads, and agriculture and jungles will be possible.

'Bioeconomy', Ministry of Economic Affairs and Employment of Finland (website). Last accessed on 23 March 2024. https://tem.fi/en/bioeconomy-and-cleantech.

'Finland – CAP Strategic Plan', European Commission (website). Last accessed on 23 March 2024. https://agriculture.ec.europa.eu/cap-my-country/cap-strategic-plans/finland_en.

12

ERVIS

Cleaning Our Oceans' Plastic Debt

Haaziq Kazi and Priyanka Prakash

OVER THE PAST HALF A CENTURY, A NEW ADDICTION HAS BEEN on the rise – the addiction to plastic. With its powers of great durability, feasibility and convenience, plastic has almost become irreplaceable. But more than half of all the plastic produced is designed to be used only once. Meanwhile, it takes plastic close to a thousand years to decompose. That means that every piece of plastic produced so far, still exists on earth in one form or another. Studies show that today we produce close to 400 million tonnes of plastic waste every year, which is equivalent to the weight of the entire human population.

In 2016, ten-year-old Haaziq Kazi, was inspired to bring about a change in the way we as a society interact with plastic. He was determined to develop an innovation that would not just reduce plastic pollution, but revive our degrading marine ecosystems. And with this passion, he designed ERVIS – the ship. Since then, he has become a strong voice speaking up for our oceans. He has shared his story through numerous talk shows and interviews. He also envisioned creating a global community of youth leaders, just like him, who together could work together to fight plastic pollution. To achieve this, he launched the ERVIS Foundation in 2019, with a goal to bring a generational change by inspiring and educating the youth to interact with plastic sustainably and responsibly.

The Plastic Problem

The IPCC report of 2021, has brought to light the urgent need for protecting our planet, including our oceans. The report suggests that extreme sea level events that previously occurred once in 100 years could happen every year by the end of this century. Changes to the oceans (including warming), more frequent marine heatwaves, ocean acidification and reduced oxygen levels have been clearly linked to human influence. These changes affect both ocean ecosystems and the people that rely on them, and they will continue throughout at least the rest of this century. This means that our oceans are crying out for help. Reducing our plastic footprint is certainly one way in which we could redefine the future of our planet.

Plastic is a universal and omnipresent material impacting our daily lives. Its specialities have addressed some of the crucial challenges for mankind. Lightweight automobile parts save fuel, improve efficiency and reduce pollutant emission. Innovative insulation material helps us save energy bills. Packaging is cost-effective and ensures food safety and reduction in food waste. In combination with bioengineering and medical-innovation, plastic implants save human life.

Due to its endless use cases, there has been a twenty-fold increase in production of plastic between 1964 and 2019, with an annual output of 322 million metric tonnes (Mt) which is expected to double by 2035 and quadruple by 2050. The current usage of plastic is based on a linear model of 'take, make, use and dispose' which is the primary reason behind depletion of natural resources, waste and environment degradation, and has adverse effects on human health.

With only 14 per cent of the plastic packaging collected for recycling, a major portion of plastic waste is either dumped into landfills, oceans or elsewhere in the environment. Each year at least 8 million tonnes of plastic leaks into our oceans. It is expected that 12,000+ Mt of plastic waste shall be generated and dumped by 2050 unless action is taken. If the current linear model continues, the ocean is expected to contain 1 tonne of plastic for every 3 tonnes of fish by 2025, and by 2050, more plastic than fish (by weight).

As an alternative to the current linear model, a circular economy aims towards sustainable utilization of resources for as long as possible and maximizes their value while in use and to recover, recycle and regenerate the products and materials at the end of their service life. The goal of a circular economic model is to implement a sustainable approach to plastic while increasing its benefits and minimizing its adverse effects to provide an environmental, economic and societal benefit. The circular economic solution proposed will help in 'closing the material loop', i.e., minimize the waste and keep it out of landfills, incinerators and oceans.

Haaziq's Journey: A Big Solution for a Big Problem

Sun Tzu once said, 'If you know yourself and your enemy, then you need not fear the result of a hundred battles.'

Born in Pune, India, Muhammad Haaziq Sarfaraz Kazi found his passion for the ocean at a very young age. Around the age of ten, Haaziq was presented with an opportunity to work on a solution for a problem he was passionate about at his school's TED-Ed club. Having watched a few documentaries about the plastic pollution crisis, he was shocked at the magnitude of the situation. Humankind has managed to taint the remotest corners of our home by choosing convenience and comfort over the well-being of our planet. He knew then that he had found his calling – to try and solve one of the Earth's biggest crises, a calamity that has been brewing right under our noses: the plastic problem.

But how would we come to solving this? One day, as he came home from playing football, his mother asked him to wash his hands. As he went to the sink to get the dirt off, he noticed how the water, when going down the drain, formed a whirlpool. An idea then popped in his mind. What if we used this same mechanism to suck all the plastic back from the oceans? He ran over to his bathtub, and filled it with some water. He then put in some objects and saw how the water created a whirlpool that brought the objects toward its centre. He then rushed over to get a piece of paper, and started drawing a circular boat with saucers attached to it, what he imagined would create the whirlpool to suck the water and filter it within the ship.

Around this time, his school had come up with the TED-Ed clubs. This was the perfect opportunity for him to work on his ship, which he named ERVIS, for a reason he can't really remember. He worked hard on it, and eventually it paid off. He presented it to his club and its members in the form of a TED talk. And as per club protocol, his and a fellow-clubmate's talks were sent to the main branch of TED-Ed.

Grade 5 started, and he had moved on from his idea. He thought he could work on ERVIS at a later date, maybe when he was older. But ERVIS didn't want to wait that long. On 14 March 2017, he received an invitation to speak live on the TED stage at TED-Ed Weekend (TEW) in New York City. He gave his talk titled 'Clean Oceans' on 17 June 2017, and that was just the beginning.

His next talk was at TEDxGateway, Asia's biggest TEDx event, which was in his home country of India, and his biggest event ever, as it was even larger than TEW. This project was beginning to gain traction. From that point onwards, he went from one stage to the next raising awareness and inspiring action for our oceans. Haaziq also had the opportunity to represent the youth by presenting the closing statement at the United Nations High Level Political Forum in 2020.

While he was being applauded at the end of one of his talks, Haaziq noticed the audience members were drinking water out of plastic bottles. And that was a moment of awakening. He realized that merely a talk wouldn't be enough to bring the desired behavioural change. People had to be inspired to walk the talk. For this, the change had to begin within oneself. One small action every day, something as small as refusing one straw or one plastic bottle, can reverse the trajectory of our ocean's degradation. Haaziq was determined to bring that transformation in mindset and inspire people to be the change they wished to see in the world.

The ERVIS Foundation: Bringing a Generational Change

The idea for the ERVIS Foundation stemmed from a very simple philosophy – if Haaziq could do it, so could other youth if given the right inspiration and platform. Over the course of three years, Haaziq had the opportunity to interact with countless young minds like himself who were passionate to change the world for the better. With a vision to create a community of global ocean advocates, Haaziq launched the ERVIS Foundation in 2019.

Registered and aligned with United Nations Sustainable Development Goals 12 and 14, ERVIS Foundation is a social enterprise that is dedicated to work against the adversities of plastic pollution. The aim is to not just educate but to also inspire the youth to bring a generational change in the way we as a society interact with plastic.

The foundation was established with three key approaches – Hero, Hub and Hygiene. The Hero initiatives encompass the short-term goals of the foundation. These primarily include the educational initiatives which focus on promoting ocean literacy and capacity building. The Hub initiatives include the mid-term goals, with key focus on driving digital engagement. These include the Zero Waste Marketplace which offers alternatives to plastic and the RoaRRR app which helps calculate one's plastic footprint. And finally, the Hygiene initiative comprises the long-term goals and moonshot projects such as ERVIS and an incubation lab which will be a space for young minds to develop their projects and innovation.

The foundation set sail in 2019 with the Hero initiative which aims at coordinating and driving awareness and communication among the youth of today so that they grow up to be more sustainable and responsible when using plastic. This journey began with the launch of the Blue Workshop programme.

The Blue Workshop sessions are designed to educate the present generation about the hazards of plastic waste and methods to mitigate the issue of plastic pollution. The workshop aims to instil behavioural changes in the way children, between six to eighteen years of age, interact with plastic in terms of its consumption and disposal. The sessions focus on spreading awareness and engaging students with activities and discussions that encourage a sustainable and plastic-free approach to life. The educational hands-on activities help children to develop an all-round awareness and understanding of the existing problems associated with plastic and gain comprehensive exposure to the adverse impacts that plastic waste has on marine life. In the first year, the foundation successfully engaged with over 1,600 students from seven schools across India and Dubai.

But every new day comes with newer challenges, and so did the year 2020. Due to COVID-19 pandemic, it became difficult to conduct physical workshops or activities. A new approach was adopted. The virtual year began with the launch of the 'For What It's Earth' series, in which experts from environmental law, marine life, plastic pollution, research scholars, etc., were invited to cater to the curiosity of the young people and enlighten the audience with the nuances of respective subject matter. The talk series witnessed the presence of experts such as H.E. Ameenah Gurib-Fakim, Dr Charles Rolsky, Kristal Ocean, Stephanie Evans, and many more.

'The Blue Circle Initiative' was another feather in the cap of the foundation. It is a purely virtual programme, under which students aged six to eighteen years undergo a three-month mentorship programme and are encouraged to develop long-term solutions for our ocean. Students from India and Dubai participated in this event. The young leaders from the Blue Circle programme went on to launch the 'Blue Warrior Club' programme. The aim of the programme is for the youth leaders to organize a club in their schools to engage and inspire their fellow school-mates and together organize, lead and implement awareness and action programmes within their schools and communities.

The club has been launched at Indus International School, Pune and Fountainhead School, Surat, in India. The two clubs launched their phase one, which focuses on ocean literacy, in February 2021 with over thirty students registering in both the clubs altogether. The clubs are currently undergoing phase two which focuses on driving action within their communities.

The foundation also has on board over fifteen ambassadors who are a part of the ERVIS Young Champion Program. The ambassadors are actively leading change and raising awareness within their communities with support from the foundation and its partners.

In the last two years, the foundation has also developed meaningful partnerships with some leading organizations and experts in the field of environment conservation. One of the key partners is the POP Movement which has greatly supported the foundation in reaching greater heights through constant guidance and collaboration. The foundation also has a strong team of young leaders and expert mentors, paving the way towards achieving the goals of cleaner oceans. In addition, the foundation also has on board Dr Ash Pachauri as the lead mentor and Cristina Gabetti as the sustainability advisor.

Our Vision for a Bluer Tomorrow

Our vision going forward is to make ERVIS a space for the youth to tinker, innovate and create solutions for the long-term well-being of our ocean. The goal is to build a global community of inspired ocean youth advocates who inspire change across different regions through awareness and action. We also aim to make ocean literacy and capacity building an integral part of schools across the globe. Our vision is to drive sustainability, reduce plastic pollution and reverse the impact of plastic pollution by bringing a generational change in the way we as a society interact with plastic.

We hope to initiate policy and advocacy level changes, by inspiring dialogues and influencing mindsets and thought processes. We will also work towards building strong partnerships and networks with organizations and leaders across the globe, with a goal to accelerate momentum of action for saving our oceans. Our ultimate goal is to inspire people to take that one action every day from now till 2050, so that we can reverse the negative impact of humankind on our oceans and revive our blue planet.

'Our planet is choking on plastic', UN Environment Programme (website). Last accessed on 23 March 2024. https://www.unep.org/interactives/beat-plastic-pollution/.

'Climate change widespread, rapid, and intensifying – IPCC', IPCC (website). Last accessed on 09 February 2024. https://www.ipcc.ch/2021/08/09/ar6-wg1-20210809-pr/.

'It's time for a circular economy', Ellen Macarthur Foundation (website). Last accessed on 23 March 2024. https://www.ellenmacarthurfoundation.org/.

'Eight million tonnes of plastic are going into the ocean each year', The Conversation (website), 12 February 2015. Last accessed on 08 February 2024. https://theconversation.com/eight-million-tonnes-of-plastic-are-going-into-the-ocean-each-year-37521.

'ERVIS Foundation Annual Report 2019-20', ERVIS Foundation (website). Last accessed on 23 March 2024. https://www.ervisfoundation.org/wp-content/uploads/2020/05/Ervis-Annual-Report_-2019-20-2_.pdf.

Ricardo Barra, Sunday A. Leonard, 'Plastics and the circular economy', The Scientific and Technical Advisory Panel (STAP), June 2018. Last accessed on 02 April 2024. https://www.thegef.org/sites/default/files/publications/PLASTICS%20for%20posting.pdf.

13

Rituraj Phukan

Assam's Global Climate Ambassador

Chittranjan Dubey

RITURAJ PHUKAN IS AN ENVIRONMENTAL WRITER, TEDX SPEAKER, adventurer and naturalist based out of Assam, a biodiversity-rich, climate change-impacted province in the north-eastern region of India. He has often represented the people of Assam and India globally in the fight for climate justice, has been an European Climate Pact Ambassador and an accredited Observer at the UN Climate Conferences (COP26, COP27 and COP28).

He is also the founder of the Indigenous People's Climate Justice Forum and serves as the national coordinator for biodiversity with the Climate Reality Project, India. Rituraj has experienced the impacts of climate change in the polar frontiers of the Arctic and Antarctic, around the Himalayas and worked with some of the worst affected communities across India. He firmly believes that the solutions have to be local. 'The planetary crises are global, but at the grassroots, most responses have to be made locally sustainable,' Rituraj says.

The diversity of the land in Rituraj's state extends to its people, with cultures and traditions of the many ethnic communities living there reflecting the natural largesse. The peace and harmony that was once prevalent did not last through his schooling years. He grew up in the middle of civil unrest; the student-led movement against the illegal immigration of displaced people caused unimaginable turmoil in society. Rituraj's own family was ostracized for his parent's political alignment during the agitation.

It was a difficult period to grow up in, and he would naively wonder why people leave their own lands and cause trouble. Fast forward a few decades, and those childhood memories resurfaced when he watched the documentary *An Inconvenient Truth*. It opened his eyes to climate change and answered questions that had lingered since those traumatic childhood years. He realized that the migrants who sparked unrest might have been early climate refugees.

His life changed when he decided to quit his government job to begin a lifelong engagement with nature. He joined the Assam-based NGO, Green Guard Nature Organization as its secretary general, working with fringe forest communities for the development of locally sustainable solutions to human–wildlife conflicts and facilitate coexistence. These initiatives included tools for human–elephant conflict mitigation, greater adjutant conservation, anti-poaching measures, awareness and sensitization, wildlife documentation and mass tree plantation. He pioneered such efforts at the grassroots level.

There were years of struggle following the birth of his only daughter, including periods of financial stress, but his wife, Rosee Devi Phukan, ensured he never lost his way. There were periods of self-doubt about his decisions and what lay ahead for the family. His mother's political career and untimely passing had a devastating effect on the family. But he and his sisters overcame every challenge that life had to throw at them.

His life took another unexpected and dramatic turn in 2012 when he was invited to travel to Antarctica as a member of the 10th anniversary of 2041 Foundation's International Antarctic Expedition. He spent several months fundraising for the expedition, which was the most challenging part as the economy was still recovering from decades of insurgency and unrest. He was persistent and finally managed to raise the funds, literally on the last day to book a spot. His first trip abroad in March 2013 was to join the life-changing expedition to the white continent. He also became just the third person from Assam and the first from the civil society to travel to Antarctica.

The International Antarctic Expedition 2013 was led by legendary explorer Robert Swan, OBE (Order of the British Empire), FRGS (fellow of the Royal Geographic Society), and the first person to have walked to both the poles. A team of corporate, academic and environmental leaders from twenty-eight countries were invited to gain firsthand experience of climate change impacts on the fragile ecosystems of the remote continent. The expedition also made Rituraj a climate activist.

'One day, we were summoned to the top deck of the expedition ship *Sea Spirit* for the Iceberg Ceremony. It was 7 a.m., and one of the coldest and windiest days I have experienced. There were exceptionally large tabular icebergs in view, which we learnt, were the remnants of the Larsen B ice shelf that had collapsed eleven years earlier,' he writes of a day in the Antarctic Sound when Robert Swan addressed them on the deck.

'Back in 2002, most people did not believe in climate change. When it started to collapse,' the expedition leader pointed across to the iceberg. 'Scientists said it would take a long time to collapse, but after the cracks were first noticed, it went down very fast and went under in less than four weeks. So, throughout the day, you will see these icebergs where they should not be. Now, you have seen climate change impacts already happening here; you must help spread the word and ensure the world leaders take decisive action before it is too late.'

On 2 March, Rituraj held up a solidarity banner in support of the Pacific Warrior Day of Action spearheaded by 350.org and the small island nations threatened with complete inundation by rising sea levels. 'My first action as a climate activist was in Antarctica!'

'The Antarctic ice sheets represent a volume of 32 million cubic km, and if melted, it would cause sea levels to rise by over 200 feet! Even partial melting of these great ancient ice sheets could inundate large parts of low-lying countries. It further opened my eyes to the vulnerabilities of low-lying countries and the likelihood of displaced people bringing further woes to poor countries, taking me back to the unrest I had seen in my childhood,' he says.

The International Antarctic Expedition opened his eyes to the threats of warming impacts and the vulnerabilities of his own region, besides opening his eyes to the solutions. The team visited the 'E-base', which is powered entirely by renewable energy and was set up by Robert Swan in 2008 to prove that it is possible to transition even in the harshest of conditions.

A few months later, he got accepted for a Climate Reality Leadership Corps training under former US Vice President and Nobel Laureate Al Gore. He travelled to Istanbul when the Turkish capital was in turmoil over the development plan for Taksim Gezi Park. Rituraj and other trainees were caught up in the police retaliation against protesters one day and had to take shelter in a house for the night after being tear-gassed a few times. 'It was a lesson that the fight to protect our environmental rights was never going to be easy,' he says.

He has been a prolific communicator of the climate crisis and its solutions, delivering over 350 presentations to date to diverse audiences in India and abroad. 'The Climate Reality Leadership Corps training helped me evolve as an effective communicator of climate change. I am proud of having overcome longstanding anxiety about public speaking and grateful for the skills and continued knowledge support in this journey,' he says about his journey as a Climate Reality Leader.

Since then, he has been invited to serve as a mentor and speaker at Climate Reality trainings in India and abroad. He also serves as the District Manager for Northeast India and National Coordinator for Biodiversity for the India branch. He was featured in the Al Gore's 2017 book *An Inconvenient Sequel: Truth to Power*.

Seeking to understand climate change in the Arctic region, he participated in an Earthwatch expedition, 'Climate Change at the Arctic's Edge' at the Churchill Northern Studies Centre in 2015. He experienced the impacts of permafrost melting on the train from Winnipeg and around the wetlands of Churchill. He participated in ongoing research of warming on the biodiversity of the region and documented the ecosystem impacts in a mesocosm and the International Tundra Experiment.

As the Chief Operating Officer for Walk For Water and Secretary General of Green Guard Nature Organization, he facilitates awareness and action on the 3W's – Warming, Water and Wildlife – working with all stakeholders including indigenous communities, students, businesses, government agencies, civil society and media for a positive societal impact. Having worked in some of the most water-scarce areas around India, he says, 'Water is the local issue of global climate change, for people and for biodiversity.'

Rituraj has worked on several impactful projects and campaigns. He was one of the leaders of the 'Hara Hai Toh Bhara Hai: Green India Challenge', a collaborative effort between Walk For Water and Igniting Minds to leverage social media's popularity to plant trees. Nearly nine million people accepted the social-media challenge to plant trees, with over fourteen million saplings planted during the first year in 2019.

Earlier, he led the Walk For Water 'Universal Safe Water Access' campaign during 2016–17 to increase awareness and action on the water crisis. The campaign culminated with nationwide observance of World Water Day at thousands of campuses and locations around India and the 'Water Pledge' being administered in over a hundred countries.

He has been a prolific writer on the interconnected planetary crises of climate change, biodiversity and water, regularly having op-eds and articles published in publications around the world. He authored the chapter, 'Climate Crisis & Biodiversity in a Warming World' in *Climate Abandoned: We're on the Endangered Species List*, a book launched in the US on Earth Day 2019.

In 2019, he returned to the Arctic as a member of the Climate Force Arctic Expedition that reunited him with Robert Swan and his son Barney, the founder of ClimateForce. Rituraj experienced the impacts of the climate change in the north polar regions, including the deaths of hundreds of Svalbard reindeer from starvation after unexpected rains froze into hard ice over the vegetation.

At Longyearbyen, Norway, he also experienced the vulnerability of humans to the unbridled power of nature. After the unnerving experience of bumpy take-offs and landings at the world's northernmost commercial airport, he saw the damage to the Global Seed Vault from flooding that had happened a few years earlier. Also known as the Doomsday Vault, it was built as a backup for humanity with millions of seeds and features to preserve major food crops for up to hundreds of years. 'Despite the herculean engineering accomplishment, high temperatures and heavy rainfall caused damage to the infrastructure less than ten years after its inauguration, and it was still closed for repairs,' he said.

He then embarked on the Reindeer Rising Arctic Lapland Expedition, travelling over 4,000 miles on public transport to engage with communities at the frontiers of climate change impacts in the Lapland region. His interest in the arctic ranges from the global weather impacts of sea ice loss to sea-level rise projections from the Greenland ice sheets and the predicted disruption of the monsoons.

Rituraj has been an invited speaker in the Stanford University, University of Alberta, University of Glasgow, Dhaka University, Glasgow Kelvin College, National Institute of Design, National Academy of Broadcasting and Multimedia, ILS Law College, IIT Guwahati, IIM Shillong, Symbiosis Institute of Management, Dr. MCR HRD Institute of Telangana, TERI School of Advanced Studies, Gauhati University, Delhi University, Chitkara University, Bhavan's College, Hansraj College, Career College, St. Edmond's College, Vikram Sarabhai Science Foundation, Assam Don Bosco University, to name a few. He was also a TEDx Speaker at the Royal Global University in 2021.

Rituraj has been invited by businesses including Oil India Limited, HSBC, Indian Oil Corporation, Bechem Technologies, Smaat India Pvt. Ltd, Indian Chamber of Commerce, and featured by media houses like *BBC Scotland*, *Guardian*, *Mirror Now*, *Deccan Herald*, Doordarshan, *CNN-NEWS18*, *CNBC*, *Outlook Traveller*, *TEN News*, *DY365*, *Northeast Live*, *DA News Plus*, *Prag News*, *The Assam Tribune*, *The Sentinel*, All India Radio stations, and the likes, with regular appearances on talk shows and panels about environmental crises and solutions.

Rituraj's interviews and articles have been published in the *American Journal of Economics and Sociology*, *Earth*

Journalism Network, *The Manila Times*, 'Journal on the Environment and Society' on Medium, *ReFrame Journal*, *Sanctuary Asia Magazine*, *Sanctuary Cub*, *Financial Express*, *The CSR Universe*, *The Christian Science Monitor*, *Eclectic NorthEast*, *Igniting Minds*, *Vanashobha* (a journal of the National Society of the Friends of the Trees), *Groundswell News Journal*, 'The Environment Management' newsletter published by the SIES Indian Institute of Environment Management.

He was a speaker at a COP28 Side Event panel on Indigenous Knowledge and Adaptation Pathways hosted by UNESCO in December 2023. Rituraj was a speaker at two sessions during COP27 at Sharm El-Sheikh in 2022 – one on climate education organized by EarthDay.Org and another on food and climate justice at a panel organized by the We Mean Business Coalition. At COP26, in Glasgow 2021, Rituraj was a 'Voices of Original People' with Listening to the Earth at the Nature Pavilion in the Blue Zone of the UN Climate Change Conference. He was also an invited speaker in a climate justice panel organized by Climate Reality UK at the Glasgow Kelvin College, and at events hosted by the University of Glasgow and The Climate Reality Project UK during the two weeks of the UN climate negotiations.

In August 2023, Rituraj was an invited speaker at the Arctic Momentum hosted by Operaatio Arktis in Helsinki, Finland. In July 2023, he spoke at the Food and Climate Shapers Boot Camp organized by the Future Food Institute in Pollica, Italy. He was also a panel speaker at the Abu Dhabi Forum on the Himalayas organized by H.E. Ólafur Ragnar Grímsson, former president of Iceland and chairman of Arctic Circle in January 2023. In September

2022, he was an invited speaker during the first Amsterdam Climate Week. During the same month, he was an invitee at the Edible Planet Summit in Perugia, Italy.

The list of awards and honours include the Environment Excellence Award 2019 for environment and climate action from IGBC, CII, Sparsh, among others; Hero of the Environment Award 2021 for environment and climate action from Kavyavarsha; Eco Warrior 202 for environment and climate action from Green Warriors Club, Hansraj College; Green Yodha 2021 for environment and climate action from Schneider Electric India; Humanitarian Excellence Award 2021 for environment and climate action from I Can Foundation; Sanctuary Wildlife Service Award 2022; Bhavartha Swarup Memorial Mahabahu Award 2023 and the Green Leadership Award 2023 in his hometown Nagaon.

Rituraj is driven by concerns over glacial loss in the 'water towers' of Asia and is currently working on an initiative to mobilize civil society action in the countries of the Himalayan region and a collaborative initiative to test technological interventions for the loss of albedo and ice cover.

He also believes in making a personal commitment to solving the environmental crisis and is vegan for the planet. He believes that a plant-based diet is a key to mitigating the planetary crises, feeding the hungry and stopping the destruction of primary forests.

Yet, Rituraj says that the main reason for hope in his incredible climate journey is the emergence of youth leaders worldwide. He witnessed the youth's power during the two weeks of the UN Climate Change Conference at Glasgow and was among the observers who walked out of the 'Blue Zone' in protest against the failure of the world leaders on the official last day of CoP26.

'In every country, young people have taken to the street, gone to court, written books and provoked lifestyle changes that has created an unprecedented momentum towards a better planet. And the most important reason for being confident about averting widespread devastation in my region is that many of these passionate and informed young people will be in leadership positions in a few years,' he says.

'Assam man to be part of Antarctic expedition,' *The Hindustan Times*, 09 October 2012. Last accessed on 23 March 2024. https://www.hindustantimes.com/india/assam-man-to-be-part-of-antarctic-expedition/story-YdGmY8SHo257kuHI4caOHK.html.

Libby Brooks, 'Hundreds of global civil society representatives walk out of Cop26 in protest', *The Guardian*, 12 November 2021. Last accessed on 23 March 2024. https://www.theguardian.com/environment/2021/nov/12/global-civil-society-representatives-walkout-cop26-protest.

Claudia Puig, 'Davis Guggenheim's 'An Inconvenient Truth (2006)', *Documentary Magazine*. Last accessed on 28 March 2024. https://www.documentary.org/feature/davis-guggenheims-inconvenient-truth-2006.

14

When Your Past Shapes Your Present

Ina-Maria Shikongo

I WAS BORN IN THE JUNGLE OF KALULU, IN KWANZA SUL, Angola at the height of the Namibian liberation struggle. My father was a commander and my mother, a young beautiful gazelle, had just freshly arrived from Namibia.

In the 1960s, the resistance against the South African apartheid regime in Namibia was ignited and led by the South West Africa People's Organisation (SWAPO). Many young Namibians crossed the border of neighbouring countries such as Angola, Zambia and Botswana to seek refuge, built the resistance and advocated for the abolition of apartheid in Namibia.

Both my parents were among the thousands of Namibians who crossed the border, and that explains why I was born in a refugee camp. Kalulu is the place where the camp was situated in Kwanza Sul, Angola. The previous refugee camp, mainly for women and children, 'Cassinga', was attacked by the South African apartheid army on 4 May 1978. Thousands died in the massacre, mainly women and children, and many orphans were taken in by the former German Democratic Republic (GDR). This is how this pogrom for Namibian orphans started.

My early years were very much about survival. We were taught as children in exile that the enemy was capitalism, so were its ideologies and member states, and that communism was the right way. As soon as we could walk, certain things became a norm, such as not talking to white people or, in case of an attack (by the South African apartheid army), staying hidden and answering to none until it became totally silent was vital for survival. This was taught to us through a fairy tale called 'Ekishi Kishi', which is a word used to describe a white monster, however one may imagine it.

In the GDR, we had to do military training: learning how to crawl in the dirt so helicopters won't detect you in case of an attack; how to survive in the wilderness and look after the wounded. My earliest memory of that is when I was six years old. Today, as an adult, I have connected the dots to why my father died when I was two years old. It was just not because of the liberation struggle that was going on. I realized that apartheid and capitalism go deeper than just stripping people's rights to their lands and dignity. The current business model is not only based on outdated practices that inspires capitalism – the oppression of people, especially indigenous communities or factory workers – but is also a system that could be categorized as the main driver behind the veil of climate collapse globally.

My passion for justice is inspired by my past. Not only my story but that of my father and the grandfathers before him. Having been born in a refugee camp in Angola and later living in a special school for Namibian refugees in the former GDR, I struggled to distinguish what the normal way of growing up is and what it's not – depending on geographies and time in history. I was taught from an early age how to say no to systemic rules such as apartheid and fight systems such as capitalism. During the apartheid regime, mining companies paid only 5 per cent of royalties, scooping away 95 per cent – which is still the case thirty years later in Namibia. If the government is lucky, they could even get away with 10 per cent.

My thirst for justice and fairness helped me express myself through poetry and books as a teenager and later through my art as well. Though I ended up studying fashion design, it made me realize that I did not want to be part of a system that systematically oppress people and nature; that's why I decided to start the Fusion Project under which I teach basic fashion design skills to grassroots communities at workshops. Eventually, I developed interest in indigenous Namibian plants and permaculture in general.

The more I learned about regenerative practices and the biggest threats, I came to know that focusing on the former was not enough. No matter how many local communities we trained, the future would still be a question mark because the biggest threat to my work and dreams was and is climate change. In 2018, a group of individuals from all age groups formed the official chapter of Fridays For Future Namibia.

In September 2020, we found out about a Canadian junior oil company that was going to start drilling for oil and gas in the Kavango region. My past flashed before my eyes. I saw myself back in Lubango in the trenches and thinking about the future of my own children. Oil brings war. Coming from the background I did, I knew that we needed to start resisting. Together with our local Fridays for Future Windhoek (FFFWHK) activists, we started mobilizing and reaching out to as many people and organizations as possible. This was also the year FFFWHK had started working with the international FFF chapter. Our chapter was blessed to have had the opportunity to meet a young man, Nic, who had a PR agency. Together with his team, he created magic. We soon had a global campaign that caught the attention of the world. This is pretty much how my climate activism started.

I know it is not an easy fight, but today I am a free Black woman living amongst Namibian white people, a privilege my father never had. Even though he was killed in a battle, today I reap the fruits of his struggle. I know that my three children will have a better future, but I will have to fight for it as my father and those before him did.

If humanity does not start treating the climate crisis as it should be treated, then we certainly risk losing our home planet. That's why voices from all spheres including policy makers are vital in the discussions around climate justice.

Capitalism or greed is the main culprit behind the climate crisis. Society keeps on feeding us with new gadgets that unfortunately do not last but require energy to function. This means more deforestation, mining, new gadgets, human rights violations, more landfills and loss and damage globally.

Our addiction to false solutions is killing the planet. False solutions are satisfying those who are craving for short-term happiness such as owning the trendiest dress from the runway, the latest iPhone, etc. The electronic companies are actually still practising slavery in the Democratic Republic of Congo with cobalt mining. The workers in South East Asian countries are still owed by big fashion brands such as Adidas. But we know that Adidas is not the only one, because this is happening in most parts of the world.

The Global South has been experiencing the consequences of greed and climate crisis for long, but the effects of climate breakdown and greed have also reached the Global North now. This greed is still a horror story similar to the slave trade that operated in most parts of the Global South. Communities are affected severely through mining, especially wherever fossil fuel production is occurring, for example, in the Niger Delta in Nigeria. In the year 2022, we have even seen rivers in the Global North drying out. Forest fires and flooding are becoming a norm. I believe environmental activism is intersectional and a step towards not just healing the planet but humanity as a whole.

The question I ask myself is: when will the multinational corporations have enough and when will humanity realize that indigenous people and their culture are crucial in the dialogue for the survival of the human race? Indigenous people still live in balance with nature. They understand their environment and know how to live from the land, unlike a homeless person in an urban setting; the one living off the land always manages to live a more dignified life. No matter how much in denial the majority of the people may be, the reality is that for most people, when they need time out, they go out into nature. Trees not only give us food, shade and clean air, but also define our mood. Nature deserves a lot more than respect.

My story is my history. It enrages me to see how a small number of people including the government use power and money to continue the oppression of the masses. Nature and humanity are dying in the name of GDP. My story is mine. Ken Saro Wiwa, the late Ogoni leader who was hanged in 1994 for defending his land against the oil giant Shell, had his story. You the reader have your story, but ultimately, we are all victims to the same god called Greed. If we look around us, we are either facing droughts, floods, mudslides or air pollution, or we are drowning in plastic and drinking toxic water as a result of drilling or industrial waste. The contentment of a few rich nations is mostly achieved at the cost of billions of people. This is the sad reality, but it does not mean that we the people are defeated. We all have the power to be a part of the change in our own capacities. It does not mean one has to start protesting and being loud, but each of us needs to find out how we as individuals can be a part of a just transition.

The possibilities are endless. It can be as simple as turning off your lights, running water and heaters when you don't use them. Being aware of the clothing and food you buy, and use your power as a customer. You have the right to demand that manufacturers make durable objects as was the case in the 60s or that they take back their packaging and dispose of it themselves. We have the power to influence policy-makers and have seen over and over again in history how the power of the people brought about change. We the people are not as powerless as we may believe. Yes, it's not an easy road at many levels and can also become dangerous sometimes.

Every fight is inspired by hope. Without hope there would be no revolutions. History has proven this time and again. A part of the reason why Namibia achieved independence was because of the end of the Cold War, but international pressure and the resistance led by SWAPO and other anti-apartheid groups in Namibia most definitely played a significant role. Another example was use of 'loss and damage' in the official text at the Conference of Parties 27 (CoP27) in Sharm El-Sheikh, Egypt. Though 'loss and damage' was removed from the agenda in the first week, because of public pressure from inside the negotiation rooms, outside of the plenaries, online and offline, it had to be added back in.

The phasing out of fossil fuels was also a hot topic at CoP27, even though over 630 delegates were from the fossil fuel industry. Vanuatu and Tuvalu have endorsed the Fossil Fuel Non-Proliferation Treaty in the year 2022, along with many other cities such as Lima, London and Kolkata. Hope is everywhere even if it may not always be visible on a first look.

Dreams can come true even if they seem impossible in the beginning. Greta Thunberg is a contemporary example of how small actions can actually lead to great wonders. The essence of the fight, I believe, is to remain pure and true to yourself. Visualize what you want to achieve. The reality is that the road is very bumpy and full of roller coasters. You learn as you take those steps into the darkness just like a baby learning to walk.

Unfortunately, one has to state that it is not safe to become an activist because of the nature of work. Companies lose millions when these projects are stopped, and they try to punish activists harshly. It is important to protect our habitats as a collective in the interest of every being – not only for the humans but the fauna and flora around us – so we can save lives. Today, we are talking not only about the lives of the defenders who are speaking up for the voiceless being murdered but also victims of floods, mudslides, wildfires, droughts – the victims of loss and damage on a global scale.

If we look back at the fight for women's rights to vote in the USA, in 1776, New Jersey became the first place in the world that allowed women to vote. But the right was revoked in 1807, and it wasn't until 1920 when US women could vote again. The struggle went on for hundreds of years. Today, women in most countries can vote, but this did not just happen in a day. It took decades and centuries of work.

Hope is in the air as more and more people are waking up to the realization that something has to change. In Florida, the elderly were severely impacted by the floods and lost everything. How are senior citizens supposed to go back to work to recover and rebuild what took them a lifetime to build?

Most insurance companies don't cover 'Natural Disasters', and yet, most insurance companies fund fossil fuel expansion, one of the main drivers behind the rise in emissions and acceleration of climate breakdown at an alarming rate. In the end, who actually wins when we look at the triangle between the investor (insurance company), the projects (fossil fuel expansion), and the insured person (the senior couple)? Without a doubt, the investor wins and the senior couple loses. A similar analogy could be drawn between the Global South and Global North, where the Global South is at the losing end.

Now, more and more people want change in their lives and are speaking up knowing that if they keep quiet, they will die anyway. So, why not die fighting for your ancestral land, clean water, fresh air and your existence.

Our biggest problem is that our current system has managed to create a divide and distort history. We know so little of each other because of what we are taught in school, which in most cases leaves out important knowledge about actual ancestral roots. We are taught to fear each other, which encourages mistrust and jealousy and can lead to extreme reactions such as racism, tribalism or other forms of discrimination.

Scholars have proven that way before Christopher Columbus sailed the oceans, Africans like Mansa Abubakar II sailed to the Americas and Asians such as Zheng He sailed there 71 years prior to Columbus, establishing Asians and other nations had already been exploring the vast oceans. Still, Africans are constantly portrayed as poor or even backward people. We underestimate the effects of colonialism forgetting that most African countries gained their independence in the 1960s unlike Latin America where Colombia was the first country to gain independence in 1810 and others followed soon after. But if we look at land and economic ownership, to this date, it's as if the colonizers never really left our homelands. Regardless of how our former colonizers see us, Columbus himself wrote in his journal that Africans had sailed to the Americas before himself.

Our job as activists is to make sure those we elect to power continue to serve the people and the planet. Politicians and big corporations do not like the truth being spoken. However, we must continue our pursuit for a safer, equitable and sustainable future.

Leo Wiener, 'Africa and the Discovery of America. Vol I.' (The University of Chicago Press, 1920).

Sharm-el Sheikh, 'Landmark Decision at Cop27 to Set Up Loss and Damage Fund', *Climate Action Network International* (website), 20 November 2022. Last accessed on 12 February 2024. https://climatenetwork.org/2022/11/20/landmark-decision-at-cop27-to-set-up-loss-and-damage-fund/.

Eric Weiner. 'Coming to America: Who Was First?', *NPR*, 08 October 2007. Last accessed on 12 February 2024. https://www.npr.org/2007/10/08/15040888/coming-to-america-who-was-first#:~:text=It%20asserts%20that%20a%20Muslim,in%20the%20early%2015th%20century.

Joseph Kahn, 'Who Discovered America? Zheng Who?', *The New York Times*, 17 January 2006. Last accessed on 27 March 2024. https://www.nytimes.com/2006/01/17/world/who-discovered-america-zheng-who.html#:~:text=But%20a%20small%20group%20of,years%20before%20Columbus%20arrived%20there.

'African King, Mansa Abubakari II Discovered America in 1312. 180 Years Before Columbus', *The African History*, 10 November 2020. Last accessed on 23 March 2024. https://theafricanhistory.com/1099#:~:text=African%20King%2C%20Mansa%20Abubakar%20II,before%20Columbus%20%7C%20The%20African%20History.

15

Learned Helplessness

An Oppressor's Tool

Yuvan Aves

April 2014

I WAS THE DORM PARENT FOR THE FIRST BATCH OF TENTH graders at Pathashaala – a residential school near Chennai, India. Two of the students stayed back in school during the summer vacations to write their board exams. While we were friendly most of the time, it was a daily challenge to meet their youthful storminess, especially with few other adults around.

The washrooms in the dormitory were serene spaces during the day. But since the school had broken for vacation and there were barely any people staying on campus, these spaces became the playhouses of bandicoot rats during the nights.

When the problem turned into a crisis, we had half a dozen rat traps bought and set up in strategic places within the dormitory. The rats were lured like thieves to gold, to the smelly coconut pieces and masala vadas we used as baits.

This way we quickly managed to do away with most of the rats partying in the washrooms. In fact, we caught all of them, except one. And this last one was a mysterious creature. We never managed to see it. But whenever it got caught in a rat-trap, the wood near the grill on the trap's roof would be gnawed away, and the rat would be missing inside. Many of our traps were laid to waste this way, and we finally gave up on trying to catch it. Now and then, the soft screeching of the tiles or a thud on a bucket would remind us of its presence. But what it was, how it looked like, how it was the only one that managed to free itself time and again, we never got to know.

A few weeks passed by. My two companions had completed their exams and had gone home. The other teachers too shortly left for their holidays. Having chosen to remain in school during the vacation, I was alone on the campus in the company of trees, birds and the skies. Then, during a late-night hour as I stood by the dorm courtyard listening to the crickets, the enigmatic creature revealed itself. There it was, creeping down the corridor, sniffing along the floor meticulously as if it did not want to miss a single molecule of air. The sole survivor of its tribe. I silently switched on a solar lamp to have a better look at this animal. It heard me and froze in its tracks. Wasn't it an extraordinarily alert creature! Its ears and whiskers twitched to the softest breeze. Its toes carried it like they bore no weight at all. I watched it without breathing. The rat then turned in my direction and began to creep towards me as it sniffed along the wall. Its eyes were milky white, devoid of any pupils, filled with cataracts. It was a blind rat. And its blindness had extraordinarily amplified the rest of its senses. I had to shuffle my feet only slightly for it to pick up the vibrations on the ground and discern my presence. Instantly, it turned around and bolted away into the darkness.

I set a trap for it again that very night, not so much to catch it but to observe its methods. Then, I lay sleeplessly shifting on my bed. This was no ordinary rat. It had survived into adulthood despite its great infirmity, in a land teeming with snakes, raptors, dogs, cats and mongooses.

When I heard the door of the trap snap shut, I leapt and ran. The caught rat was scratching around inside the wooden box. It could not comprehend what it had run into. It only knew that it felt the cold air from above through the grills. Catching onto the metal grill with its tiny paws, it gashed its incisors on the grainy wooden edge of the roof with a frenzy. In no time, it had chipped away enough of a gap, climbed out and thrust itself into darkness again on muffled feet.

Why didn't the other rats do the same? Some of them were much bigger and brawnier, with front teeth like chisels. They could have cut through steel if they had wanted to. Why didn't they attempt to escape, the same way as their blind comrade?

Research by American psychologist Martin Seligman throws light on the behaviour of these rats. Taking Pavlov's methods a step forward, Seligman gave mild shocks to two groups of dogs which were free within a small barricaded space over which they could jump over and escape the discomfort. In the first group were dogs who were subjected to these shocks for several days while they were tied on a leash. They could not escape their fate. The second group was not subjected to any shocks previously. When dogs from the second group were put in the closed space and given a shock, they immediately jumped over the barricade and ran away from the hostile stimulus. But the dogs from the first group, those who were already conditioned by the shocks, tolerated and accepted the maltreatment even though they had an opportunity to escape. They had 'learned to remain helpless'. Seligman called this behaviour 'learned helplessness'. It is a strange case where getting used to bad treatment curbs one from liberating oneself even when there are opportunities.

How much of our realities are we merely accepting as given without attempting to participate in it? Another famous psychologist, Daniel Kahneman, said the mind thinks that 'what it sees is what there is'. But what we 'see' is susceptible to all kinds of conditioning.

So, considering the blind rat who stalked the washrooms at night, its disability freed it from the conditioning the rest of its troop was under. It escaped because it could not see the trap. It escaped because it never knew it was trapped.

October 2020

I am returning to this essay about six years after the episodes described in it took place. I am still a teacher but no longer part of a closed community. By I have been a part of several campaigns, rallies, and social and environmental movements. The world is in its post-COVID-19 era. During the months of lockdown, the entire public was preoccupied with the safety and health of family and self. Millions of migrant labourers struggled with loss of income, food shortage, and the journey back home. Health workers globally strived day and night to fight the disease outbreak, attending to the ever-increasing number of cases. These were the ground realities. However, the authorities took it as an opportunity to pass several anti-people and anti-environment pieces of legislations and decisions. It began with forty environmental clearances given to industrial projects in protected areas, in a single meeting of the National Board for Wildlife in April 2020. Streets – the main canvas of peoples' campaigns – were closed. The draft EIA 2020, an overtly corporation-friendly notification that put the ecology at risk, was put out for public review during this time of medical emergency. Mining reforms followed as another windfall for industries. The amendments to the farmer laws were pushed through, opening the agricultural sector to private players, bringing in free trade policies and taking off the government's responsibilities regarding market and price regulation. The FCRA law was amended with increased compliance requirements. This period of public suffering was fully utilized. Meanwhile, in response to the right-to-information requests made by people asking for data on the number of migrant labourers and health workers who died during the pandemic, the government said it had no data – in violation of one of its most basic responsibilities of accounting for the deaths of its citizens.

Oligarchies, authoritarian governments and oppressors of all kinds strive to create collective 'learned helplessness'. They subject people, by design, to more and more injustice, inequity and abuse – so that they may grow numb, so that their voices tire, till such a way of being becomes the new unquestioned normal, and solidifies into the customary structure of society. Psychology of this field tells us that when the 'outcome-response independence' is internalized by the victim, it is extremely hard to unlearn it. Geopolitical analyst Eszter Nova wrote, 'Oppressive regimes thrive on helplessness. A population reduced to helplessness is docile and passive – even when it is outwardly loud and belligerent. Its symptoms include the dissolution of individual perspectives, active inaction, as well as the onset of a survival mentality.' This phenomenon needs recognition as a tool of despotic and hierarchical social and political systems. Strongly vertical and bigoted power-structures need it vitally. Another psychologist, Mathias Sager, has said, 'Even small daily exposures to oppressive structures of economic and political/social environments influence people's psychological internalization of observed superiority and inferiority. Conforming behavior provides the necessary practice to develop the tendency to obey the 'unavoidable' orders of oppressors in a learned 'helpless' manner.'

Massive dissent to the centre's capitalization of the pandemic was largely spearheaded by youth movements across the country such as Fridays for Future India, Yugma Network, Adivasi Students' Forum, Let India Breathe, Extinction Rebellion, etc. This daunted ministers and public authorities. It made them push policy-review deadlines further, cancel some clearances related to national parks and wildlife sanctuaries that had been approved, and slap terrorist laws on youth groups. These events gave reason for hope and worry. Had the collective 'older public' gotten used to the maltreatment? Had they turned into the first group of dogs in Seligman's experiment? In my own experience of rallying in public spaces and collecting signatures – against a coastal road which threatened a beach and would displace fishing communities, a metro station project which sought to replace the few green parks left in Chennai, a port which would decimate a biodiverse lagoon – in general, it is the youth who are forthcoming in giving their solidarity and joining the cause. The net older population prefers to ignore or walk away, sometimes leaving one feeling embarrassed for campaigning.

The philosopher J. Krishnamurti once said, 'It is no measure of health to be well adjusted to a profoundly sick society.' The capacity and space to dissent is a good societal health indicator – something the larger political scenario of India is impoverished in right now. Dissent-space is a two-way political thermometer. It shows that the individual in society is active, questioning, sensitive and alive. And it also indicates whether governance is listening, learning, concerned and open.

'Learned helplessness' and 'imposed social incapacitation' can create cultures bearing centuries of atrocities. They can establish deadly status quos and spaces of loaded, brutal silence – which act as their reproduction chambers. The caste-system prevalent in the country reflects this glaringly. How did such an inhumane, irrational system root itself so deeply? Who gets to classify human beings? What political soil perpetuates such a practice? Such questions face difficulties in their collective emergence when their subject has been so thoroughly mainstreamed.

The dehumanising violence against Dalit and Adivasi people, the subjugation and exploitation of women, the normalised disenfranchisement of religious minorities, and state-sanctioned eco-cide in the name of development: these norms are social inventions, not natural order. Opposition to them is met with autocratic measures and manipulation from the powerful. Across these realms, tragedies and crises catch public attention for a while. They may even shift status quos. But the rest of the time, silence is a temporary convenience privilege provides – to those who have it.

To find all means to inoculate ourselves against learned helplessness is indispensable for a ground-up climate of democracy and humane society. To do this also means to be responsible ancestors. To resist it, is to hold hope in the way Rebecca Solnit describes it, 'an ongoing series of acts of defiance'. Against the injustices we see outwardly of course, but perhaps more importantly defiance towards and within ourselves – to becoming habituated, to the temptation and facile comfort of indifference and silence.

Eszter Nova, 'The Role of Fear and Learned Helplessness in Authoritarian Thinking. Interdisciplinary reinterpretation of the underlying thinking patterns of authoritarianism', *International Relations Quarterly*, Vol. 10, 2019.

Martin E.P. Seligman, 'Learned Helplessness' (University of Pensylvania, 1972).

Daniel Kahneman, *Thinking, Fast and Slow* (New York: Farrar, Straus & Giroux, 2011).

Mathias Sager, 'The Psychology of Political Helplessness', Medium (blog), 22 February 2019. Last accessed on 1 April 2024. https://mathias-sager.medium.com/the-psychology-of-political-helplessness-b323242383f5.

Jiddu Krishnamurti, *Commentaries on Living* (New Delhi: Penguin Books India, 1968).

Rebecca Solnit, *Hope in the Dark* (London: Canongate, 2005).

Vijaita Singh, 'FCRA amendments crippling our work, say NGOs', *The Hindu*, 09 March 2021. Last accessed on 02 April 2024. https://www.thehindu.com/news/national/fcra-amendments-crippling-our-work-say-ngos/article34521449.ece.

16

Loving Nature

Desmond Majekodunmi

WHILE WORKING IN NAIROBI AS A MUSIC ENGINEER AND producer thirty-five years ago, I was so impressed by the way the Kenyans worked in harmony with nature to drive their economy – which was based almost entirely on agriculture and eco-tourism – that upon returning to Nigeria I decided to become a farmer. So, I took a crash course at the International Institute for Tropical Agriculture (IITA). One day, after reading an inspiring book on agriculture practised in India, I met the author of the book in the cafeteria, a certain Dr Khan, who through his research had developed a disease-resistant variety of cassava, one of our staple crops, that helped avert a major food crisis. I was highly motivated by Dr Khan, and he was to be the first of two Indians who influenced me to become an environmentalist.

My second Indian eco-motivator was Dr Murthy, one of the pioneers of the Indian agriculture revolution who catapulted India into food and agricultural raw material self-sufficiency post-independence, after a particularly exploitative colonial intervention. I had acquired a stretch of land on the outskirts of our rapidly expanding capital city of Lagos, and from the lessons garnered from Dr Khan, I had started an agro-forestry system on the rather fragile coastal soils of the city. However, I was using quite an intensive chemical-based farming system. Providence led me to meet Dr Murthy, who was doing some consultancy work in Nigeria, at a social function. He expressed an interest in visiting my farm, and when he came, I was totally blown away when he took a tiny taste of the soil and was able to accurately analyse its approximate acidity level. He advised me to adopt organic farming practices as this was far more harmonious with nature. He said that to farm sustainably, it was imperative to work with nature and not against her, as was the practice at that time in many of the Indian farmsteads. This was really my first introduction to the value of conservation, and I'll always be grateful to these men for embarking me on my journey to environmental activism.

I encourage my Indian brothers and sisters to continue on their journey of self-sufficiency, as they are on the path to developing into a truly great nation. However, they would be advised not to sacrifice sustainability on the altar of profitability and to attach more value to their traditional practices which I believe hold nature and her creatures in very high esteem and encourage a harmonious relationship with Mother Nature.

My next influences came soon after establishing my Khan/Murthy inspired agro-forestry farm which incorporated patches of farmland amongst the existing rain forest. This little piece of original forest was able to maintain quite a rich biodiversity and avifauna. As it was quite close to the urban centre, it soon attracted bird watchers from the Nigerian Conservation Foundation (NCF) who were closely linked with the British WWF. The bird watchers were delighted with our agro-forest, and I soon became a member of this pioneering conservation NGO, where I currently sit on the governing council.

Over the years, the NCF were able to persuade our government to establish an environment ministry and develop a national parks agency and currently stands as the foremost conservation NGO in West Africa. Soon after joining the NCF, I realized that protecting nature was very important and kind of cool. In fact, it was so cool that my late wife Sheila, whose amazing singing prowess has been duly acknowledged by the likes of Stevie Wonder and Mick Jagger, and I decided to record an album *Green Leaves* which was dedicated to promoting the cause of conservation with tracks such as 'Mother Nature' and 'Green Leaves'. I'm not a very good singer and as dear Sheila had been endowed with a hundred per cent perfect pitch, she was very sensitive to any little off note, so I was relegated to playing some guitar, doing a few backing vocals and rapping, at a time when rap had just emerged on the music scene. Till today I'm still known in some circles as 'Papa rapa'.

A few months after releasing the album in Nigeria, Prince Philip, the then Duke of Edinburgh, and at that time the President of the WWF, visited Nigeria as a guest of the NCF. Sheila and I performed some of our songs for him and presented him with the album. He was very appreciative and wrote a letter recommending us to Richard Branson who at that time was still running his first major company Virgin Records. We headed to London, but the negotiations with Virgin didn't work out as we refused to compromise with our 'green' agenda and do more commercial music. After a few small shows in London, we headed back to Lagos and our farm, where we performed our green music at several massive festivals at Lekki Beach, a huge venue that I was operating at that time. From the consequent reactions, we were delighted to observe that many folks were influenced to take up farming and better environmental practices. However, one of Prince Philip's sayings stuck with me, 'The conservation of nature, the proper care for the human environment and a general concern for the long-term future of the whole of our planet are absolutely vital if future generations are to have a chance to enjoy their existence on this earth.' This really inspired me to become a more dedicated environmentalist, especially since we had now started to see more aberrant weather patterns being caused by anthropogenic global warming, as well as an increasing extinction of species and destruction of habitat. It was becoming obvious that something was becoming seriously wrong with the environment.

Ironically, it was when I was in London during the 2009 G20 conference that I heard a speech by the Duke's son, now His Majesty King Charles III, as he was hosting the world leaders, that I became an environmental activist and have since dedicated my life and resources to the cause of protecting nature. The words that moved me so greatly were, 'If we lose the battle against climate change, we shall be bequeathing unto our children a *poisoned chalice*.' The implication of this horrendous inheritance to our beloved children struck me hard.

When I got back to Nigeria, and even though Sheila had now passed on, I threw myself into the battle with extra vigour. I converted my farm into a park, Lekki Urban Forest Animal Sanctuary Initiative (LUFASI), and made 'Loving Nature' our motto. Here, we encourage visitors to enjoy the health benefits of being in a green space whilst persuading them to have a more caring attitude towards the environment. We also run environment workshops for students of all age groups and have hosted thousands of people over the past few years. Apart from embarking on lecture tours and TV and radio appearances, I have personally mentored quite a few young people who are now making great strides in promoting the cause. Recently, I've started trying to persuade religious leaders to pick up the creation care gauntlet and preach it from their pulpits, with the admonition that being a good steward of the environment is a common injunction in all major scriptures. I believe that the laws of karma and retribution are inviolable, and we are already seeing nature's reaction to our destructive ways. The recent pandemic and terrible weather occurrences are certainly loud warning signs that we're putting our house on fire, and we *must* undergo a renewal of our minds to transform us into beings with a far more caring, loving attitude towards nature and each other before our selfish, greed driven actions trigger off irreversible and totally catastrophic consequences. However, I am optimistic that faced with the dreadful consequences of not doing so, we shall develop, before it's too late, a *loving nature*.

H.R.H The Prince Philip, *The Environmental Revolution: Speeches on Conservation, 1962*-77 (A. Deutsch, 1978).

'Prince Charles repeats call for urgent climate change action', Climate Home News (website), 07 January 2013. Last accessed on 1 April 2024. https://www.climatechangenews.com/2013/01/07/prince-charles-repeats-call-for-urgent-climate-change-action/.

17

Reflecting on Extinction Rebellion and the Future of Climate Movements

Rupert Read

IN MY ASSOCIATION WITH THE CLIMATE MOVEMENTS, I HELPED launch one of the biggest climate and ecological movements of our time named Extinction Rebellion (XR) in the autumn of 2018.

At XR, I played the role of a political strategist and spokesperson. But now, I have moved on from the organization. I have come to believe that the best compliment we can pay to the partial success that XR had, in raising climate-consciousness as never before, is to lead consequential movements through the 'Overton Window' that it has wonderfully enlarged.

We need more and more mass climate movements. To achieve this I have co-created and support an emerging movement under a new name 'Moderate Flank'. However, retrospectively speaking, XR played a great role in my involvement with furthering climate action and activism.

When I was young my aunt took me on a 'Save the Whales' march, but what truly inspired me to begin campaigning was a period of living in the USA. I thought I had seen a glimpse of the future, and I really didn't like it. The endless consumerism, materialism, wastefulness, the everyone-for-themselves attitude, the blatant disregard for people and the planet was prevalent and soon wasn't limited to the America of the 1980s.

It was then that I decided to spend my life trying to turn the tide – as an academic, in local, national and international politics, as an author and by being part of Extinction Rebellion at the time.

Like many who are aware about the climate nightmare, I have cycled through periods of despair on the one hand, and desperate hope against hope on the other.

We have veered between not seeing how we can possibly make it through the long ecological more-than-emergency, and being tempted to give up.

However, after so much time, I think we have to be clear that we are fighting against mass extinction of species on this planet. That's crucial. The brutal truth is that things are now almost entirely certain to get a lot worse for a very long time to come and mitigation is the best we can hope for. It's a brutal and depressing realization but one that is necessary. To set aside all the hopes I'd cherished my entire adult life for us to really *win* still leaves me with an enduring grief.

Of course, that doesn't mean giving up. Far far from it. We clearly still need to fight for change, not least in reducing deadly emissions. We are fighting for our lives.

But part of what mitigation really means now is the literal meaning of the word: which is simply making things less bad, not making things brilliant.

We have now arrived at our last attempt, and it's the last chance to do something – anything – about the situation we find ourselves in.

When I first started airing my concerns and worries so publicly, I was worried that I would be called a defeatist, a traitor, an alarmist and that indeed the actual real-world effect of my truth-telling would quite likely be to demoralize the very activists who most need bucking up. But it turned out that my worries were misplaced.

The calling-out I feared hardly ever happened; instead, people resonated with my message. And that segued right into the launch and growth of Extinction Rebellion, as one stream amidst the flood.

Far from being condemned to a lonely isolation, I found my gang. And it was soon a massive gang, changing the world. The moral? Telling the truth *works*. Being authentic is a superpower. Being present – to the reality of the climate and ecological emergency – is a superpower.

Whereas pretending that everything is going to be fine is in the end nothing but a recipe for burn-out.

The XR has guarded against burn-out culture from the start: by seeking to create a regenerative culture.

Although I am not one of the co-founders of XR, I have been involved since before it was launched on the public stage. We have pushed many Western governments to declare a climate emergency and have brought thousands of people around the world on the streets to be part of climate movements and we should feel proud of them, but I feel there is so much more to come – especially when more people join the vast wave of climate movements of which XR is a part.

Consumer boycotts, voting and so forth is not enough – we must undertake non-violent direct action. Small gestures of disobedience and defiance can create a spark that catches light and ignite a much, much larger rebellion. We need governments that put our health, well-being and shared ecological security before the interests of big business and the pursuit of endless economic growth.

As a society, we need to work on our ability to share, to care, to have fun, to communicate and to think intelligently and creatively about our own futures. It is about people before profit, surely, but it's so much more than that.

It's about rebuilding broken communities, but not under the thinly veiled guise of nationalism or isolationism. It's about recreating community, being compassionate to all living beings and our planet, in the here and now. Much of what is to come cannot be managed at a bureaucratic level. What might work in one place may need to be modified entirely in another. It makes sense to let people on the ground control what happens and when. We need to encourage them to care for their neighbours.

The same applies for food and energy production; not having to rely on vast, uncertain, polluting supply systems but to have these essentials home grown makes sense in every way you think of it.

Only if we approach this with honesty about what is and is not possible will we have any realistic hope of seizing the chance that lies before us.

The goal is not a glorious utopian total victory, rather it is survival.

For a gentle as opposed to a dire descent from our current height of civilizational hubris.

For wise adaptation to the climate and ecological decline baked into the next generation.

Everything is in place in a certain sense for us to make the kind of change that we need to make. But it seems that we're unable to do it. Of course, one of the main reasons we're unable to is simply the enormous power of those interests that are in favour of upholding the status quo.

And that's where Extinction Rebellion comes in. When we join forces, we can bring about a great shift in consciousness.

But there is a great sorrow that we need to go through: that the great transition we had hoped for has not yet occurred. Such that there will be great suffering in the years to come. But when we *experience* the great sorrow, when we allow ourselves to *feel* our grief, then a great energy becomes accessible to us. That is what powers us, in our rebellion against extinctions. That is what shifts consciousness. And then shifts, if you will, reality itself.

Our lives and those of so many others are in the balance. The greatest challenge humanity has ever faced is now.

Be part of facing it.

Only if you do so, will you be able to look your children in the eye.

'What is XR?', Extinction Rebellion (website). Last accessed on 23 March 2024. https://rebellion.global/about-us/.

18

Resilience 2020

A Story of Maize, Quash and Beans

Iván Ransom Rodríguez and
Kevin Morales Münstermann

MALCOLM GLADWELL HAS SAID: 'IDEAS, PRODUCTS, MESSAGES and behaviours spread like viruses do.' Three rules need to be fulfilled to make the spread possible. A few people with rare social characteristics need to be involved, the message needs to be impactful and the right social context is required. Probably this is the reason why today's youth climate movement is showing results although it isn't the first time that climate strikes are organized by youth. Today's urgency is making some realize that we need to fashion things in a different way, although doing it isn't precisely an easy task. It is essential to challenge everything we have learned and look for a new and more sustainable way to do it. Sometimes it will be policymakers who need to develop a law or a rule to make sure that everyone follows it. It could be a company's decision to change their processes or products or the society avoiding products and services that don't fulfil the environmentally friendly requirements. Or, it could be all of the above. But what happens when we are living within a big lie or a set of many lies?

The odds have been somehow against us, and it is for this very same reason why Resilience 2020 was born. It isn't the first environmental project either, but in just a year it has shown a unique potential to challenge the lies. Two resilient young Mexicans, Kevin Morales Münstermann and Iván Ransom Rodríguez, who were born the same year humanity crossed Earth's tipping point on carbon dioxide in the atmosphere, came up with a solution that could put our societies back in the right track. The story of Resilience 2020 couldn't be told without considering theirs.

Kevin's Narrative

Two years ago, I was at the hospital fighting for my life against a bacteria called *Streptococcus pyogenes*, a flesh-eating bacterium, main responsible of rheumatic fever. I had been in such bad health for a while. For months, I had a bad cough but had no time to see a doctor. Like most people, I also avoided what was important and focused on what's urgent. As the co-founder of a soccer academy called Academia Borussia, I was involved in using sports to bring about social change, but neglecting my health on the side. This was ironic because we promoted sports and good health. While I was lying in bed at the hospital feeling the most intense pain that I had ever felt, I saw in the news that the youth were on the streets shouting, 'No more climate injustice.' I was feeling sorry for myself, until, suddenly, a childhood dream made its way into my mind. My dream in life had been to save the world, especially the animals in it. My love for nature comes probably from my family, because we have always adopted pets. We usually spend summer holidays in Germany. Near my family's hometown was a beautiful forest called Deister where we used to go often. To me, this felt like stepping into paradise – everything was so different there compared to my daily life in the severely polluted Mexico City. I wanted to bring that paradise back home but didn't know how. I thought that by becoming a vet I could save wild animals injured from human activity. But later, I changed my decision and studied biology instead, because I didn't want to save just an individual animal but the whole planet. The problem with my dream was that in real life defining who's the villain isn't an easy task. Everyone could be one and yet it was no one at the same time. I tried to become the hero that my dream required.

When I was around eight years old, I quit sodas, candy and fast food, and decided that I would be a vegetarian. I disliked the idea of harming animals but couldn't stop eating animals, because my parents told me that I could eat whatever I wanted when I reached age eighteen, but until then I had to follow my family, which owned a meat and pizza restaurant. Probably since then my health became less important for me. I allowed the daily stress of life and society to change me. Therefore, lying in bed at the hospital, I realized that the system is the villain, not the people. It changed me and could do the same for anyone. I promised to myself that I would become the hero that I always wanted to be and being vegan was a starting point. On the third and last week at the hospital, I was so scared that my life would be the same as before, and that everything that I promised to myself wouldn't happen, that stress and daily life would win again, that I didn't want to leave at all. It seemed like a safe place. Luckily, right after I left the hospital, and against all odds, I became vegan. Feeling so powerful for being able to change my life in one day, I asked myself what was next. I thought that the next step would be to change my own home, so I installed many eco-technologies. It was expensive, but it felt amazing. Unfortunately, not everyone has the money to get them, and for the sake of the people, the economy, and the environment, this needs to change. In January 2020, I sent a letter to my parents telling them that my next task would be to start a business that would allow people to afford the eco-technologies. This matter somehow led me to the second World Sustainable Development Forum (WSDF) in Durango, where my background in biology and international relations alongside my entrepreneurial experience set the grounds to fulfil the promise I had made to my parents. But it didn't happen with me alone.

Iván's Narrative

To be precise, it was the wolves that brought me here. I was lucky enough to grow up surrounded by nature. Ever since I can remember, I went to the forest in Durango, Mexico, my home state, every weekend. As I grew up, I knew I would end up devoting my life to protect nature, particularly animals. When I started my studies in biology, I was committed to preserve the Mexican Gray Wolf (*Canis lupus baileyi*), however, I was told since the very beginning that by the time I finished my studies, this subspecies would most probably be extinct. So, I thought it would be better to dedicate my life to protecting many species instead of just one, and the best way to do it would be to fight climate change. To do so, I focused on cellular and molecular biology, using which I would be able to reduce pollutants in the air and soil through phytoremediation. But life is full of surprises, and after a story of hard work and a series of 'high risk, high reward' decisions, I ended up in the master's programme in sustainable development at the University of St Andrews. After I finished my studies, I returned to Mexico looking for a job and for a way to bring about change for good, but time passed by, and no one hired me. After years of despair, frustration and self-doubt, I found light in the most unlikely place – Durango. It was in my very own hometown which I had left 15 years ago, where I ended up meeting the Protect Our Planet (POP) Movement, and specifically Ash Pachauri, the man who changed my life forever.

Stories Overlapping: The Day Streptococcus and Canis 'Met'

If hearing our stories didn't feel like déjà vu, wait till you read about our 'first' meeting.

We were at the WSDF in Durango, both on our own, spending the whole day amazed by the panellists. Both of us decided to seize the opportunity and overstayed, looking for a chance to meet them. We ended up at the same table with the panellists. Kevin's face seemed very familiar to Ivan, but he couldn't figure out why, until the former started talking about the nopal cactus and its biotechnological properties. That conversation seemed to ring a bell as well for Ivan, so he assumed that Kevin was a biologist. After connecting all the dots, he remembered that a common friend introduced them years ago at the university. In that moment, we reconnected, shared our stories and decided to work together to pursue our common goal.

Weeks later and back in Mexico City, we met at a coffee shop. Kevin brought back his idea of installing eco-technologies, but there was something missing to make it a feasible business model. That is where Ivan came up with the idea of integrating eco-technologies into a circular economy system that would connect people from the cities and rural areas in a way in which the former's residues could be valuable resources for the latter. That was the game changer. And so, in that precise moment on 13 March 2020, Resilience 2020 was born.

Growing Together: Of Diversity and Support

Industrial agriculture promotes monocultures, which means growing the same plant on the available surface. This intensive system depletes soil's nutrients, and sometimes even uses clone plants, which make the crops vulnerable to plagues due to the non-existing genetic variability – if one falls, the rest will follow. That's one of the reasons why diversity is so important for species survival.

At the beginning of Resilience 2020 we were like a monoculture, just two biologists trying to build something that was way beyond their expertise. The first obstacle that we faced was creating a video for our project. None of us had any experience whatsoever, but then our beloved POP family came to the rescue. Ana and Michael from POP made a colourful and dynamic video in which we explained the basics of the project and shared our contact information. The need for a diverse team was more than evident, and we needed to take that step forward as soon as possible if we wanted our project to grow with the urgency that our planet needed.

Have you ever heard of the Mayan milpa? It is the way in which the Mayan civilization has been growing their crops for millennia. There is maize, which provides support for the beans and allows them to access the light by reaching heights that would be impossible for them to reach alone. Beans then promote atmospheric nitrogen fixation, making it available in the soil for other plants. Then there is quash, whose wide leaves prevent solar irradiation from reaching the floor, and, in this way, they create a beneficial microclimate for plants and other life forms in the soil, as well as prevent nutrient runoff by helping to maintain soil structure. An analogy can be made here in our lives where the POP Movement is the maize, Borussia Dortmund is the quash, and we are the beans (no pun intended!). These three plants also provide a wide variety of nutrients for the people – what a difference in comparison to industrial agriculture, right? As we described above, diversity and mutual support are paramount for species survival, and that same principle applies to successful working teams.

Though when we began on March 2020, it was just the two of us, since then we have received invaluable support from the POP family. Within a few months, more people started to join in to work with us. David, Alma, Kevin and Ivan had to multitask and do mostly everything in 2020, relying upon their basic understanding of other disciplines. They managed to consolidate the project's structure and present it, with Humberto's invaluable contribution, to national and international audiences. We won our first award in the category of 'Outstanding Project Idea' at the International Conference and POP Festival for Youth-Led Climate Action in 2021. In December of that year, the team was almost complete, and we were able to consolidate three departments: Research and Development, Design and Marketing, and Finance.

In the following year, 2021, we began to expand our project. To build a team spirit in an online environment can be challenging, especially for people who have never met before, but somehow, we managed to do it. Soon enough, strangers became friends and family, and we've had many adventures as a team. One of our most cherished moments comes from a trip to Zapopan, in the state of Jalisco, Mexico. After months of hard work from the Research and Development department, Brisa and Estefanía from Design and Marketing delivered pure excellence in Resilience 2020's master document, which opened the door for us to have a meeting with the city's government. We spent the eight-hour journey nervous about the meeting next day. The hopes, trust and hard work of the whole team was in our hands. Our performance needed to be at the highest level to honour the months of hard work that led us all there. It was going to be our first meeting with a politician, and we needed it to be perfect. Dafne along with José Luis Bravo (our partner from PES Prospectiva S.C., a consulting firm dedicated to addressing complex problems across public and private sectors) played a crucial role in that. It was a decisive meeting with Graciela de Obaldía, Zapopan's Interim Municipal President. We reached an agreement that fetched support for our project and set the ground for launch in Jalisco, one of the states with the highest GDP in Mexico.

Resilience 2020: A Win-Win Project

Resilience 2020 was born not only to address environmental needs, but also to tackle social issues such as inequality. Therefore, we installed five eco-technologies for free at homes, which allows people to save money and improve their quality of life while decreasing their environmental impact. Through a greenhouse, households produce their own food. The *humus* produced by the compost is used to nurture their plants. A water-harvesting system is also installed to supply the greenhouse. The solar heater reduces fossil fuel gas consumption to heat water used in baths. And the most important eco-technology that we install is the biodigester, which is considered as the future of renewable energies. The *biogas* produced in the biodigester replaces fossil fuel gas consumption for cooking, and the *biol*, an organic liquid fertilizer which is also produced there, is integrated into our circular economy system. Resilience 2020 buys the latter and sells it to farmers at the price of the cheapest synthetic fertilizer on the market. This allows farmers to transition to organic production without increasing their costs. Some of their now organic products are bought by Resilience 2020 under a fair-trade scheme and sold back in the city. The *humus* is used on a similar scheme.

Resilience 2020 goal is to change the way we all produce and consume. We aim to reduce food insecurity through the greenhouse, water scarcity through the water-harvesting system, and promote clean energy usage through the biodigester and solar heater. Moreover, we reduce air, water and soil pollution by separating organic residues from the inorganic ones at the source, which in turn facilitates recycling. And finally, through organic production, we also reduce impact on biodiversity associated with agricultural lands. This is a starting step, however, more is needed to be done. Resilience 2020 also provides constant training to maximize benefits from the eco-technologies, and produces organic and biodegradable cleaning and cosmetic products that are sold at the cheapest price on the market to make them affordable for everyone.

Our call for action is a call for love

We ought to live by every day to make our ephemeral existence one that is worth living for.

Resilience 2020 is not just the result of 1 year, 6 months and 25 days of work, but of the choices of our lifetime, and of the people that have believed in us and supported us all the way through. Our call for action is to gather, to support others, to build networks and help others to connect. To celebrate and protect diversity and to be open to hear, to learn, to grow. Join projects in your community, join global efforts or create your own path for the change that is so urgently needed, every bit of help matters and is a step in the right direction.

Unfortunately, the last IPCC report suggests that our civilization has only this decade to bend the carbon emissions curve. Otherwise, we will be on a path of no return towards greater climate extreme events which will threaten our species survival. We believe that Resilience 2020 success would be an important contribution to this cause due to its great impact and potential to becoming a global project. We are currently seeking for expansion inside Mexico, in midterm we will reach other countries, and before we reach Earth's deadline, Resilience 2020 will be at a global scale.

Malcolm Gladwell, *The Tipping Point: How Little Things Can Make a Big Difference* (London: Little Brown, 2000).

'Página de Inicio', PES Prospectiva (website). Last accessed on March 23, 2024. https://www.pesprospectiva.com/PAGINA-DE-INICIO/.

Hannah Ritchie, Veronika Samborska and Max Roser, 'Plastic Pollution', Our World in Data (website). Last accessed on 23 March 2024. https://ourworldindata.org/plastic-pollution.

19

We Are Many!

Climate Activism in Germany

Annemarie Botzki

I REALIZED EARLY ON THAT NATURE CONSERVATION WAS important. As a child, I often played at my neighbour's house. There was a large poster on her door. It had impressive, dark green trees. Vines. The eyes of a jaguar peering out hidden between the leaves. Next to it was a bare field, with only a few sad tree stumps left in the ground. Above, the writing stated: 'Every minute an area as large as a football field of tropical rainforest is cut down.'

Rainforest. That already sounded magical at the time. Lush green and exotic animals. Water vapour. A forest, different from the one we had here in Germany. It must have been important and of course, a place worth protecting, that much was clear to me. For a long time, I trusted that such magical places, such as rainforests, would be protected by humanity. That there would have been laws against their destruction. It has been 26 years since I first stared at that poster in shock. Deforestation has proceeded tremendously since then, exactly as described on the poster.

Although I can remember that exact moment and my horror, the experience did not make me an environmentalist. School, study and travel came before that happened.

The moment I realized that I had to help stop the destruction came many years later. In 2015, the year when Nepal had been hit by a destructive earthquake, millions of Syrians had fled their country, and the Volkswagen emissions scandal had been exposed, the UN climate protection negotiations were taking place in Paris at the end of the year.

I was there, reporting on the negotiations as an energy journalist. It was Friday afternoon. The world's most renowned climate researchers had been invited to a lecture in an inconspicuous room. The climate negotiations should have been concluded by then, but the proposed draft agreement was met with a lot of criticism. The 1.5-degree target had not been mentioned yet, although more warming meant many people and countries would die.

So, that afternoon I was sitting in a room with around 50 other listeners from across the world, attending the lecture with headphones and simultaneous translation. Scientists were discussing how coral reefs worldwide would bleach and die with 1.5°C heating. They made it clear that irreversible tipping points would trigger the planet to heat up exponentially, like domino stones falling.

They clarified the existential threat climate heating posed to people and ecosystems. They referred to several studies, showing one graph after another. They warned that the 1.5-degree target needed to be urgently included in the Paris Agreement.

I looked around this room full of international journalists and participants. They stared at the panel with headphones on their heads, sitting quietly, unmoving.

I, on the other hand, was seething. Why had I not been aware of these devastating effects? As a diver, I was shocked by the gloomy prediction that the beautiful coral reefs would die. Of course, it was even more unnerving because a billion people worldwide depended on living, healthy reefs for income and food.

I felt like crying. The gloomy prognosis had hit me like a wave. I was stunned by the extent of the destruction that lay ahead for humanity. The grief, resentment and anger that I felt were overwhelming. How could have the governments around the world been so irresponsible with our planet? How did we allow ourselves to arrive at such a dangerous point?

But this anger and shock were also liberating for me. Because if governments did not and could not protect us, we needed to do it ourselves, I realized. It gave me courage and energy.

I decided to become a part of the change and take the responsibility. I realized it was one of the most meaningful things I could do with my career, time and life. Before, I had been looking for meaningful work; now, I had found an existential task.

A few days later, on Sunday, the Paris Agreement was adopted to limit global warming to 1.5 degrees and decarbonize our economies by 2050 (the net zero goal).

This was a milestone. The Paris Agreement became an international treaty signed by almost every country. I called my editor in the London office and told him about this landmark agreement. But there was only guarded hesitation on the other side of the line.

Many years have passed since this treaty was signed, but the importance of the net zero target is yet to sink in with most. The certainty of this goal for human civilization has not penetrated equally. It sounds like just another nice political goal. But the far-reaching impact on our economy is not clear to many.

The most important questions I have been asking myself since my participation in the Paris Climate Conference 2015 are: How can we as societies convert our economic systems and our everyday lives? How can we live without new emissions? Who will build this world? Who will stop the coal, oil and gas industries? Who has a plan to completely change the way we live?

I have been pondering upon these questions for several years. These questions have changed my life. The more I realized the danger we have been heading towards, how little time we have and how profound the change we need is, the more determined I have become to find answers to these questions.

I quit my job as an energy journalist shortly after the Paris Conference. I moved from London to Berlin to work at a new start-up in the solar industry. I have been conducting research on innovations in renewable energy and have joined the climate movement Extinction Rebellion.

Many people think Germany is a green and environmentally friendly country. But the truth is that we have some of the largest fossil fuel industries pushing hard against the change we need to protect our environment. The powerful car industry relies on oil. Meanwhile, chemical giants such as Bayer produce dangerous pesticides and coal companies such as RWE, (formerly, Rheinisch-Westfälisches Elektrizitätswerk Aktiengesellschaft) the German multinational energy company, destroy villages across Germany to burn more coal.

The government will only change if people demand it. Nothing will happen unless people stand up and protest, take legal action and increase the pressure.

One of Extinction Rebellion's demands is, 'Tell the truth and act accordingly.'

The governments of the day have known about the consequences of the climate crisis and the destruction of ecosystems for decades, but they do not stop it. They have been holding negotiation on the climate since 1995 (the so-called 'CoP negotiations', of which there have already been twenty five). And yet, emissions worldwide have risen by 60 per cent since 1990. That's why we need to rise up.

I have seen the large changes a few ordinary people can make. From stopping a precious forest from being cut down and preventing water wells being sold off to global corporations to forcing stoppage of the coal industry. It was people like you or me who accomplished these.

Under the aegis of Extinction Rebellion, more than 6,000 people came to Berlin from all over Germany in the autumn of 2019 to make it clear that they were prepared to engage in civil disobedience to finally get the government to act. Inspired by icons such Mahatma Gandhi and Martin Luther

King, we have sat down on streets to block the never-ending traffic. To demand a change right then, right there.

However, the efforts of the climate movements were greatly impacted by the coronavirus pandemic. But we also achieved some important goals because of it. Since then, many people have realized that the climate crisis is about survival. The European Union declared a climate emergency, climate targets were strengthened, and democratic participation has grown considerably (so-called citizen assemblies which has been one of Extinction Rebellions' demands).

But much more needs to be achieved, of course. The laws need to be changed, for example. One campaign I ardently support is the call for an ecocide law. Because I am convinced that corporations or politicians who destroy nature on a large scale, as agricultural corporations do in the Amazon, or oil companies, should not be allowed to get away with it. That's why I'm campaigning for an ecocide law that would punish such behaviour. This would have global consequences and would deter companies from furthering the destruction of our livelihood, because they could be held personally liable for it.

So, what does the world I fight for look like?

I hope we can together create a new world with cooperation, courage, and trust, and preserve a habitable planet. We can make forests recover and meadows flourish. We can strive to grant all the people access to organically grown food, and drive through inner cities for free. We can build houses that produce more energy than they consume.

We can aim for a world that creates safe harbours and healthy coasts. Where refugees find fulfilling work in cooperatives. Where women in solar networks install solar panels on every sunlit roof. Where wind turbines float on the ocean. Where we consult together in citizens' councils on how to reduce emissions even faster.

We will not be able to stop the rising ocean. But we can choose to do everything we can now to help regions affected by erosion and rising sea levels while sustainably transforming coasts. This could entail building CO_2-negative cement for sea walls, promoting healthy mangrove forests, and harnessing wind energy, with all of these creating many new sustainable jobs.

It would be a world where a sense of justice would be held dear. Where those that destroy the planet for profit would face jail time. Where the fossil fuel companies would pay for the damage they have caused. The communities that have lost their homes or health would be the first to get access to solar and wind energy.

We would start with a global conference to negotiate how to shut down the fossil fuel industry. Churches, insurance companies, communities and universities would pull their investments from coal, oil and gas companies. Billions of dollars would instead go into clean energy and cities instead.

Asthma would become less common, and so would heart attacks. Premature births would be reduced because traffic and air pollution would go down. The cars we book via app would drive quietly and be charged with clean electricity. The fine particles that we have been breathing in for decades would all but disappear.

We would work for three or four days in a week. We would have time to work in community gardens. To go for walks. To shop at markets. New neighbourhoods would emerge. We would understand each other better. We would get to know our neighbours. When we breathe, we'll feel a little calmer. We would know we are prepared for stronger storms, hotter summers, and rising sea levels. Our coasts would be protected. Our forests would be recovering. Clean solar energy would be produced on every rooftop. Agribusinesses would have been transformed into community-based cooperatives. Organic would be the standard. We would readily repair our clothes, shoes, bicycles, televisions and telephones. Our library would have a wide range of tools, machines and electronics that we could borrow.

Our town would be green and flourishing. But we won't just care about our cities. We would recognize the damage corporations have done around the world and send patent-free technology, money and support to communities worldwide.

The challenges are great. The good thing is, you don't have to face them alone. You are not alone. We are not alone. We are many.

'The Paris Agreement', United Nations Climate Change (website). Last accessed on 23 March 2024. https://unfccc.int/process-and-meetings/the-paris-agreement.

20

Environment in Cultural Context

Sachchidanand Joshi

CERTAIN ANCIENT SCRIPTURES ARE TREASURE TROVES OF knowledge. One of the earliest known texts to mankind, the Vedas are derived from the Sanskrit word 'vid', which means to know, and contain a wealth of information on an array of topics. Knowledge pertaining to our environment, our cosmos, also forms a vital part of our texts, and we are fortunate to have inherited this pool of knowledge as part of our textual heritage. These texts have numerous allusions to the hydrologic cycle, environmental conservation, ecological balance and other related topics. The meticulously recorded details that have been sustained over the centuries demonstrate the high degree of understanding that the seers and people of that age held.

In the *Atharv Veda* (Atharveda Prithvi suk [12]), it is said 'Maata Bhoomi Putroham Pruthivyah' (the earth is my mother, and I am her son). Additionally, for the morning prayer one is supposed to recite 'Samudra vasane devi, parvatatastan mandale, Vishnu patni namastubhyam padah sparsham kshamasmve,' (*Atharveda* Prithvi suk [12], while putting their feet on the earth for the first time in the day. It can be translated to: O' mother earth please forgive me for putting my feet on your chest. One text known as the 'The Pruthvi Sookta' which is as old as the Vedas elaborately explains the relation between man and nature.

The concept of Panch Mahabhoota (five elements) elucidates the deep bond of human soul with nature. The five elements – Fire, Water, Earth, Air and Space – are also the inseparable elements of human body. The connection between the elements creates an equilibrium which also creates the ecological balance.

Texts such as the Ramayana, the Mahabharata, the Upanishad, the Puranas, the Smritis and, of course, the Vedas establish the cultural connectivity with the environment. The use of various materials in different rituals is also based on the principles of the environment. The Yagya (Havan) and the materials used to conduct one are believed to be beneficial to the process of environmental cleansing. The worship of different trees and animals in certain traditions does not have ritualistic significance, but it aims to preserve the environmental balance.

Several ancient texts are environmentally conscious, and their ethos has passed down to the generations in the form of beliefs, folktales, rituals, observances, festivals and pilgrimages. Indian communities such as the Bishnois of Rajasthan are to reckon with when it comes to protecting the blackbuck and the khejri trees in the region. Another example of living sustainably can be seen in the ancient agricultural practice known as *halma*, which is practised in the tribal communities of Madhya Pradesh's Jhabua District. Here, majority of the families in a village gather their tools and work on one person's land on a certain day. Every household is eventually covered in due course. Although the equipment and tools are privately held, the whole community benefits from their use. Ultimately, the land is collaboratively farmed, while the products are privately owned, ensuring a significant decrease in the cost of production methods due to common tools and equipment being used. The effectiveness of this method has demonstrated that organising community around concerns of environmental regeneration, management and protection of natural resources is possible.

Animals, birds and fishes are all revered in Indian philosophy. The admiration and affection for environment have been extensively depicted in literature and scripture, such as in the 'Panchatantra'. Along with sacred groves and woodlands, a variety of animals, including the garuda, lion, peacock and snake, have long been associated with our culture. The upkeep of particular areas of land or woods as 'sacred groves' devoted to a deity or a local god that are safeguarded and worshipped, is a traditional practice based on religious beliefs that has profoundly contributed to natural conservation. Such sacred groves are found all over India, and they exude power and tranquillity.

Conservation of water is also deeply integrated in our culture as can be noticed in the affinity to refer to rivers as mothers or goddesses that nurture mankind as well as animals and plants. Most of the water bodies present in

India have been associated with a divine origin, and their sacrality is upheld even in present times. Rivers such as Ganga and Yamuna are often depicted on the entrance of temples. Nature also finds its manifestation in our paintings, sculpture and architecture to remind us of its importance in our lives.

To celebrate and revere the bounties of nature and magnificent environmental phenomena, humans created many festivals. These festivals take the form of harvest festivals and pilgrimages in Indian culture. Moreover, the entire length and breadth of the country celebrates such festivals. Though the names vary across regions but the essence behind them is similar. Any festival in India is loaded with numerous layers of convictions or customs. Festivals celebrating harvest are no different. Harvest festivals, which are observed all over the country and even the world, are all about gratitude. The celebrations are intended to encourage us to express gratitude for a crop that can provide food and support for life. In India, whether it is Makar Sankranti, Pongal, Lohri or Baisakhi, the aim is to respect food or *ann*. There is an understanding that a coordinated and seamless fusion of natural factors and thoughtful human intervention is the key to obtain a good yield or harvest. The farmer is always aware that all of his efforts and abilities can be for naught if nature decides to wreak havoc. Similar to this, even with the richest natural resources, crops cannot be developed if the farmer does not, among other things, till the soil, plant seeds, care for them and understand the dynamics of his cropping patterns. As a result, harvest celebrations encompass much more than mere manifestations. It's about a deeper conviction and a mutually beneficial relationship that benefits thousands of people. As a result, harvest festivals serve as a reminder of how nature and humans collaborate to produce the most fundamental necessities for survival. Mutual respect is especially evident during India's harvest festivals. The sun and other natural forces that are necessary for a good yield are revered. Food is offered to the gods, and everyone shows respect and gratitude. Even though farming is predominantly a rural activity, harvest celebrations are nevertheless often observed in metropolitan cities as well. The fundamental principle is generally known and honoured, despite the fact that cultural and societal undertones and manifestations may differ.

Our harvest festivals are a concoction of musical extravaganza, dance, rituals, traditional cuisines and communities coming together adoring their traditional attires and partaking in the celebrations together. If we conduct a survey of the most celebrated harvest festivals of India, one would realize that the whole of India reverberates with festivities showcasing gratitude and joy for the harvests. Harvest celebrations come in a number of styles depending on the season. Location-specific harvest festivities have different dates. Harvest festival festivities, which usually have a specific local flavour, are strongly rooted in the local culture and history. Different harvest celebrations embody various facets of the local custom and culture. Some festivals signify the start of a new year in many cultures. For instance, in Tamil Nadu, the new year starts with Pongal which marks the beginning of the auspicious Tamil month of Thai. Ugadi is a new year celebration in Andhra Pradesh, Telangana and Karnataka.

Apart from honouring the bountiful harvests, Indian culture also has a historical tradition of observing the change of seasons in the environment. The onset of the spring season is celebrated as Basant Panchami in the whole of North India. All these festivals are based on their local harvest season. Those regions which are involved in agricultural practices plan their respective harvest seasons. The festival of Lohri signifies the end of winter and the beginning of a new harvest season.

Makar Sankranti is one of the most important harvest festivals in India. Per the legends, this festival marks the end of an unfavourable phase and the beginning of a holy one. Particularly in villages of Gujarat, Kerala, Tamil Nadu, Haryana, Himachal Pradesh, West Bengal and Punjab, people celebrate the harvest of new crops with a bonfire, carnivals, songs, dances, kite flying and rallies.

People of Punjab and Haryana celebrate Baisakhi or Vaisakhi to thank god for a good harvest. People wear their most colourful dresses, sing the happiest songs and dance to the melodious beats of the *dhol*. It is the most loved harvest festival of Punjab. Baisakhi fairs are also organized where acrobatics, wrestling, *algoza* and *vanjli* performances can be seen which makes it one of the most interesting harvest festivals celebrated in India.

Ladakh Harvest Festival brings to fore the Buddhist traditions concerning the symbiotic relationship between man and nature, and this has gained immense popularity and fame all over the world. Ladakh looks bright, beautiful and absolutely stunning with the commencement of this harvest festival. Monasteries and stupas are decorated and pilgrimages to Thangka of Kyabje Gombo are mandatory as a part of this celebration. Archery along with old social and cultural ceremonies and art and handicrafts are other features of the event. The Ladakh Harvest Festival is celebrated in Ladakh, Zanskar and Kargil. Dramas or 'Chhams' are performed to display life and teachings of Buddha and different dance forms of Tibetan culture.

Lohri is a renowned folk harvest festival in Punjab that showcases traditional dance and songs. To kill the chills of winter, the entire family and neighbours gather around the bonfire and sing together and offer grains, corns and nuts to respect and appreciate the grand harvest of sugarcane crops.

The onset of the spring season is celebrated as Basant Panchami in the whole of North India. It is an auspicious day that is associated with the colour yellow. One can see the magnificent mustard crop fields in the countryside, especially rural areas of Haryana and Punjab. Indian dishes *peele meethe chawal*, *makke ki roti* and *sarso ka saag*, that are in sync with the nature during this time and are relished as part of the auspicious celebrations.

Moving further on, the North Eastern states of India have a hearty list of harvest festivals which enrich the remarkable Indian culture of commemorating the riches of nature. The very famous harvest festival exuding pure bliss and cheerfulness is of Bhogali Bihu. Every year in January, the entire state of Assam showcases enthusiasm and delight in celebrating Bhogali Bihu. The farmers of Assam celebrate and cherish the efforts of cultivation and reap the benefits. The celebration starts one night before with Uruka – the community feast. On the day of Bihu, the *mejis* or pavilion made of clay and hay are burnt. Local women wear stunning *mekhla*s and participate in group song and dance. Also known as Magh Bihu, this is an exotic festival and a vibrant name on the list of harvest festivals of India.

Wangala is the merry celebration of a 100 drums played by Garo tribes of northeast India. This is one of the popular harvest festivals of India marking the onset of winter. During this festival, the sun god is worshipped with immense devotion and zeal. Women wear their traditional colourful clothes and dance during this harvesting festival, while men rhythmically drum their fingers on the traditional drum pads.

The inhabitants of Khasi Hills worship the goddess Ka Blei Synshar and celebrate the plentiful harvest with vigour and excitement. Ka Pomblang Nongkrem festival brings ultimate joy and happiness to the community. The celebration comprises animal sacrifice and Nongkrem dance with a sword in one hand and yak-hair whisk in the other. This festival is quite popular among the people of Meghalaya and is widely celebrated.

The Dree Festival is among the most famous festivals in Arunachal Pradesh as it marks an important time of the year for the Apatani tribe – the harvest season. Characterized by sacrificial offerings and prayers, Dree is celebrated on the 5th of July every year in the Ziro district of Arunachal Pradesh. The festival is celebrated with utmost joy by people of all walks of life who dress up in traditional clothes. Locals perform traditional dance and music numbers while others enjoy a feast of tangy rice and millet beer. Other than this, the three-day festival is also marked by various games and sports that the locals and onlookers are entertained with. The entire ritual is carried out to pray before the four gods – Tamu, Harniang, Metii and Danyi –

so that the Apatanis can be blessed with a bountiful harvest season.

Nuakhai is an age-old harvest celebration in Odisha. Locally 'nua' means new and 'khai' means food. This is not only a popular harvest festival but is also celebrated to appreciate the passing of the past and evil days while welcoming the new and beautiful with open arms. The festival is also known as Nuakhai Parab or Nuakhai Bhetghat.

Gudi Padwa is a grand harvest festival of Maharashtra marking the beginning of an auspicious new year. People make rangoli designs at the entrance of their homes and decorate them with flowers and a handmade doll. Folks meet friends and relatives, exchange wishes, and cook sweets such as *puran poli*, *shrikhand* and *sunth paak*.

Nabana is another crop festival of India celebrated during the paddy plantation harvest. This is one of the most celebrated traditions of Bengal, in which new rice is harvested with sheer joy and stocked in homes. Farmers from Bengal cheerfully participate in this harvest ritual in the Bengali month of Agrahayan and offer the first grains to Goddess Lakshmi while thanking her for all blessings. West Bengal Tourism has taken initiatives to welcome tourists from around the country for the celebrations.

Onam is a harvest festival celebrated with great enthusiasm in different parts of Kerala. The festival is celebrated for 10 days with the arrival of Mahabali. To relish a successful harvest, the people decorate the entrance of their homes with floral rangoli, wear new traditional clothes, cook delicious food and celebrate with traditional music and dance.

Pongal is another name for Makar Sankranti, which is celebrated at the same time in various cities of Tamil Nadu. This is a thanksgiving celebration where people express their deep gratitude to mother nature for the produce of the year. This is one of the most colourful harvest festivals that is celebrated over four days. It is amongst the most popular festivals of Tamil Nadu.

Ugadi is a regional new year celebration for the people of Andhra Pradesh and Karnataka. This harvest festival is considered auspicious to start new work and ventures. On the day, local people take an oil bath, wear traditional clothes, decorate homes with earthen lamps and rangoli and perform Ugadi puja at home.

Grand worship of Lord Vishnu or Lord Krishna, elaborate family lunch, evening prayers and fireworks sum up the complete picture of the Vishnu festival. This is an interesting harvest festival celebrated on the first day of the Malayalee New Year. Women of the house prepare Vishukkani – varieties of traditional cuisine to offer to gods – with rice, golden lemon, golden cucumber, jackfruit, yellow konna flowers and betel leaves.

Residents of Mumbai enthusiastically celebrate Agera, another agricultural celebration. It celebrates the beginning of Maharashtra's harvest season during which Catholic residents 'thank God for the abundance of blessings received' and is observed on the first Sunday of October in the cities of Mumbai, Thane, Raigad and Vasai. Also known as 'Thanksgiving Sunday', it is marked by a festive parade with dance and music to the nearby paddy field where a priest blesses the property and gathers a few sheaves. The sanctified paddy is ultimately carried to the food booths outside the churches before being distributed among the attendees. The land and crop are blessed by one of the priests. And then, the rice stalks are taken to the church with sounds of the village band in a *palki*.

Kottiyoor Ulsavam, or the Kottiyoor Vaisakha Mahotsavam, an annual pilgrimage spanning almost a month (27 days), is one of the most popular festivals in Northern Kerala. It is celebrated in the hills of present-day Kannur in Kerala, situated on the banks of the mighty River Baveli. The 27-day annual pilgrimage commemorates the mythology of Daksha Yaga. The celebrations takes place in two temples: the Akkara Kottiyoor and the Ikkara Kottiyoor. Akkara Kottiyoor Temple is the main venue. Interestingly, it opens annually only during the festival days. Over the 27 days, the devotees worship a self-created (Swayambhoo) idol of Lord Shiva. The rituals include pouring of ghee (Neyyattam); bringing of a sword from Muthireri *kavu* in Wayanad; Elaneer Vayppu, where tender coconut is offered to the idol; and finally ends with Elaneerattam, in which the head priest pours tender coconut water on the idol. This 27-day festival is a visual treat, with nature playing a prominent role during this divine occasion.

Rubi Rana, 'Environment in Hinduism', *International Journal of Sanskrit Research*, 2019.

'From Lohri, Makar Sankranti to Pongal; here's how India celebrates these harvest festivals', *Mint*, 13 January 2024. Last accessed on 23 March 2024. https://www.livemint.com/news/india/from-lohri-makar-sankranti-to-pongal-heres-how-india-celebrates-these-harvest-festivals-11705128312988.html.

21

Climate Voice from Uganda

Annette Atugonza Nabirye

NOW A CLIMATE REBEL, A BUSINESS PARTNER, WIFE, MOTHER and a mentor to many youth groups, *I am Annette.* I was born in Fort Portal, in the south-western part of Uganda where my late single mother worked as a public servant in the ministry of works. I received my primary education in six different district schools because of my mother's routine transfers. It was too unfortunate that both of my parents could not survive HIV/AIDS, and I highly curse its existence to date.

After the death of my mother, I had to live with my late father, five stepbrothers, three stepsisters and three stepmothers for the remaining years before moving out for my higher education.

During my school time, what we usually studied about the environment was always pertaining to how to keep it clean and understanding that planting trees helps in rain formation. Other effects such as carbon absorption, etc. were not necessarily discussed. Later, during my higher education, I learnt more about pollution and understood that if we litter environment with products made from plastic, it will destroy our soil.

During my university days, along with my younger siblings, I started to discover a lot of new things, and one of them was the Internet. It had reached many regions in the world before Uganda. I chose to study computers during my BBA at Makerere University, Kampala.

Through different online networks, I kept volunteering for long before getting employed as an aide, which was my first job in a publications company the *Daily Monitor*. I volunteered for UNOHCHR (Office of the High Commissioner for Human Rights), and we traced and rescued girls in areas of rural Tanzania who were victims of female genital mutilations. I also worked remotely to help farmers in Maharashtra, India, who were committing suicide because of crop or seasonal failures due to climate change.

I had already started to notice crop failure at my late mother's village in Hoima. My grandmother could never get good harvests of rice out of her gardens. She almost got nothing after months of guarding her plantation chasing away birds whose food was preferably the same rice which she was growing for herself. That experience appeared to me as a struggle for food between human beings and those innocent birds that could only respect 'scare crows'.

I kept thinking more about how to be useful, contribute and maybe to do something to save our environment and spread awareness in my country. I researched online for environment-related content and came in touch with the Extinction Rebellion website.

I noticed there was a spirit of independence in what one could do after reading through the demands, principles and values of the Extinction Rebellion. They seemed unique and different compared to many other environmental movements.

From that time, I chose to be more responsible in all that I did – shop less, use environmentally friendly items and utilize any space I could find to address people, especially the youth, asking them to get involved and take action. In my free time, I decided to study more through edX about climate change, piracy, governance of water bodies, and conducting research on sustainability.

As a mother of four boys, I often look beyond myself. I think about how the future of my children and my grandchildren will be on this planet considering the ongoing climate crisis. This makes me want to do more and spread more awareness so that the future of my kids and others can be saved. I am a woman, and we are the ones who suffer the most due to adverse climatic conditions.

Today, African women from the indigenous communities are forced to vacate lands full of natural resources so that rich foreign investors and local businessmen could profit. This leads to mass migration, and they are forced to relocate to terrible places far away from their motherland. I am talking specifically about women who are uneducated and from indigenous communities who are deprived of their basic rights. Because when natural calamities happen, they don't know where to go for help. They are often the primary caretakers of their children and by the time help reaches them, it is already late as infant kids can't wait too long without milk and food. Also, due to corruption, it doesn't reach them, on time. Men are given more priority than women due to the patriarchal mindset in our culture. There are regions like Karamoja, Bundibugyo and Bududa in Uganda that experience frequent natural calamities, leading to pests, diseases and malnutrition among children and women.

We need to reform our education system, and we need to teach our children and our societies at a very early stage about ongoing environmental damage. It is not until people go to school and pay a higher fee that they get to know about climate change. As an individual, I am trying to spread awareness in my community, family, neighbourhood and city as well as do online advocacy. It is not necessary for everyone to take radical action on the ground. We can find different ways to spread awareness based on our own circumstances.

Today, climate refugee camps in Uganda and in Africa are peopled by babies, teenagers, adults and old people, who have no access to clothes, food and medicines. You will see hundreds of people staying in congested rooms. These refugee camps are dominated by men who discriminate against women. They openly exude favouritism and only support their families and relatives. They try their best to amass all goods and services from the NGOs for their own benefits. They also have too much influence on the activities of these NGOs. Government-assigned authorities in charge of the camps steal tangible donations that were meant for female victims. They sell it outside the camps and line their pockets. At an individual level, I have spoken against them many times, but not to much avail.

The great push behind my activism comes from all that I see in the lives of these female climate refugees. First, they need healthy food for their children. Often, I hear them saying, 'We want medicine and soap first for the children, even if you do not give us this or that… please give these first.'

I am advocating against the use of plastic bags in Kampala, but it is not an easy task to convince people to stop using it. The plastic bag manufacturers are a big mafia who have already stocked up massive supplies of plastic bags. Even if today the government bans it completely, it will take a couple of years before it vanishes from the market. The nexus between local businessmen and the government is too strong to be broken to stop the use of plastic completely.

I don't think that the environmental campaign should be only at the society level; it should start right from the family, because family gives birth to society. If we teach kids at family level, they don't need to wait to go to school or college or go to lectures on the environment at government or elite organizations to become environmentally conscious.

The policymakers in Uganda can be real game changers, but they rarely do anything. They have access to all information and resources, but they don't do anything to stop the climate crisis. They have the authority, experience and opportunity to stop this genocide, but instead they take different routes for their capital gains.

Policymakers have access to foreign investments, and they are aware which companies are going to destroy their native lands, but still they allow it to happen. The countries of the Global South and their decision-makers need to unite to stop this loot and destruction being carried out by the Global North. For centuries, the Global North has been destroying the Global South – first through colonialism and now through neo-liberalism and neo-colonialism. The post-World War institutions were built for their benefits only, and we from Global South are still paying a heavy price.

The bitter truth is that in East African countries we have regional imbalances in rural and urban development. Most of the population seems to be relocating to urban centres, ending up with less sustainable service delivery and they still go to live in slums around these centres. Once they migrate from rural to urban landscape, they need to start their life afresh without any support from society. They live on the sides of streets without running water and sanitation and unfortunately many generations are lost to come back to a normal life which they earlier had in their rural villages.

The education system in Uganda or in countries like Tanzania and Kenya should be revisited as it is dominated by the health (medical, pharmaceutical considerations or lobbies) sector with lesser focus on the environment. There is still space for wide broadening in areas of environmental management and conservation-related careers, courses, engagements, studies or even government-driven campaigns.

Governments can exploit the existing trust in cultural and religious leaders, institutions or spaces in general to have more awareness creation, practices about the need to plan for climate and ecological crises at the level of hosting the affected communities.

I have also come across some activists and campaigners pretending to be environmental protectors whereas their involvement is only worth a dollar. I call them commercialized environmental activists or advocates. It is very unfortunate to see these people polluting this sacred environmental space.

I think we need to care more for and love the animals around us. This doesn't mean I want to see them next to my tent, but I do not want to kill them or encroach on their space and just let them live their normal life. We need to embrace their freedom and ecosystem.

Talking about hope, if the issue of the environment becomes an essential centre point of the knowledge imparted to a child from the day it is born until the highest level of education is obtained, we shall have hope for our environment. At the moment, there is unprecedented environmental damage going on. The only good thing is that many individuals, scientists, indigenous communities, environmental protection bodies and social movements have realized that somehow, they need to come together, and they have started raising their voices

From Uganda, I personally call on everyone regardless of our differences in culture, colour, class, region, religion, education, health, wealth and marital status to jump on the wagon and take action so that we can save our planet!

'What is XR?', Extinction Rebellion (website). Last accessed on 23 March 2024. https://rebellion.global/about-us/.

22

Lighting Fireflies

Nicolás Eliades Vesga

ONE BY ONE, ALL THE FIREFLIES ARE BEING EXTINGUISHED. During warm summer nights, a child would gleefully wrap himself in their life-giving glow. Once upon a time.

Now, thirty two years on, I struggle to see them, those fiery flies.

I was working as an international communications specialist in Spain when Pachamama called me to her service. At that point, I was labouring for someone whose primary purpose was to make money off the back of worker ants.

In this employment, I was numbed by a false sense of dedication and purpose. I managed to convince myself that I was indeed doing good work, contributing to a better planet through water councils. It was at this point that the bullying started, courtesy of said employer; a product of a toxic reality which ultimately placed profit over planet.

My boss disdainfully asked me to fill in a form for him to attend a climate-change training seminar in the German capital, hosted by the Climate Reality Project. I filled the form, much resentfully. I was angry with him, with myself, and with the world. I had gone from director to despicable, because of, well, ego.

I thought to myself, 'Why shouldn't I go, too?'

With his form sent, I snuck mine in too.

My form was accepted. My boss's wasn't.

Shit. Now what?

I pleaded with the organization to invite him, too. They did.

June 2018: I found myself in a hall in Berlin at the seminar. Gawking and listening to former US Vice President Al Gore unpack where our planet was at. What a delightful stroll down a litany of everything that was wrong with our society, and its impact on our climate. Terrifying fact after terrifying fact.

I didn't actually feel sick. I felt stupid. Ridiculous. For a hot decade there I thought our leaders had this sorted.

I mean, we've known about such crises for… what? Forty-odd years? For crying in a bucket, I remember studying about the greenhouse effect at school in New York when I was nine. Ms Grandstone told us all about it – back when there were still fireflies.

Back in Madrid, I watched my boss rubbing his hands at the prospects of new clients he would attract with the Green Gore noddy badge he bagged in Berlin. I was frankly disgusted. Despondent. Desperate.

Done.

It was then that I vowed to myself – never ever will I crawl back under capitalism's whip again. Betrayed by hope,

I vowed to honour my constant prayer, 'Gaia, make me an instrument of your peace.'

In the ancient world, hope was seen as a vice.

One of my native languages, Spanish, offers a window into this ideology (you see, I tend to think in English while I feel emotions in Spanish).

If I express hope for something in Spanish, you would be forgiven for thinking I am waiting for it. Take 'Espero al bus.' I 'wait' or 'hope' for the bus. What the person hearing understands depends on the inflexion.

Hope hides inaction. Depends on inflexion. And I was done with waiting. It was time to act. Or not to be. But how?

Then it hit me. I'm a comms man! 'You do communicating dude, do that. Your flavour of magic!'

The Climate Reality Project was my first port of call. I flew to Bilbao to deliver Al Gore's PowerPoint on the existence of climate change to an energy company that supplies my gas. I deliver the presentation. They clap. They go back to work. I fly back.

Then a few weeks later, Annika, a good friend from the University for Peace (in Costa Rica, where I did my master's degree), called from Minnesota. 'Nic, I'm coming to London soon, on 17 November, for the weekend. Hop on over and let's have that reunion. It's been 15 years since last we met…'

I bought a cheap flight ticket to London for that weekend, (cause that's what we did in 2018, we, without resolve, hopped on those fossil-burning machines and without thinking flew to where we needed to be, for a weekend). Why not distract myself from deciding upon the purpose of my existence?

Then, Ro called.

I had met Ro one happy night on the streets of Madrid, my sometimes hometown, some two years ago.

'Hi Nic, you good?' crooned Ro, Irishly. 'Was just calling 'cause I want to share something I think you need to be a part of… I'm currently in London… a group of us have just set up a movement... Extinction Rebellion or XR we are calling it

'We want to bring people from all over the UK to participate in non-violent civil disobedience. You know, like Martin Luther King. We want to disrupt financial life in the British capital and draw attention to the climate emergency. With love, but hitting where it hurts.

'Let's fill the jails with peaceful, artful protest; no one else is doing anything, right?'

Right.

'Whatcha doing November 17? We're planning an action, blocking bridges. Central London. I'll send you the info, good if you could join us. We could use an international comms eye like yours.'

Hungrily, I read all the docs Ro had sent. The declaration of rebellion; this was the world I wanted.

Three demands – truth, immediate reduction and more democracy. A goal.

Ten values. A guide to align us. Contrarian as I may be, I was compelled.

That's how I found myself on Lambeth Bridge, along with hundreds more of my kind, birthing a rebellion to life, lest we became extinct.

Meanwhile, not far away, in Poland, a Swedish girl chastised global leaders for dereliction of duty in the face of an emergency. She was speaking at the Conference of the Parties (CoP), edition 24. The traditional United Nations' 'carnival' where world leaders punt true climate action over the cliff.

Back in Spain, Ro put me in touch with some other folks who were keen. Six of us huddled together, shivering in a cold dark room, just off Gran Via, Madrid's iconic thoroughfare. January 2019. 'Let's help organize the rebellion in Spain.'

We pool magic, talents, trades and gifts.

My mission was to establish a communications commission for the nascent national Spanish chapter to communicate climate and non-violent direct artistic action, carried out by 'rebels'. And persuade society.

A handful of folks with an interest in communications, and I, together created a working group – esXcomunicaR.

In Spain, the not-so-distant ghosts of a dictatorship mean civil disobedience doesn't come easy. So you gotta flow. For many, including myself, this was the first time we dipped our toes into disruptive activism.

We began by blowing *vuvuzela*s (an African trumpet of sorts) and miming at busy pedestrian crossings when the light was red.

Steadily, we graduated to blocking a garage entrance at Spain's oil and gas corporation, Repsol. April 2019. Unperturbed by us, employees just used the other gate instead.

esXComunicaR managed to splash some headlines across national media. Not the big ones though. Not yet.

Meanwhile, back in London, XR UK was bolting pink boats to Oxford Circus in festivals of life and love for the planet and each other. Soon after, the UK parliament declared a climate emergency. Nominal maybe, albeit a small victory nonetheless.

The truth-telling had begun.

It had been the hottest March on record.

Thirsty for similar national truth back home, esXcomunicaR issued a press release calling on all of civil society to rally around a solitary undeniable reality: the need for a national declaration of a climate and ecological emergency.

With press release in hand, NGOs were called left, right and centre. And not just the environmental ones. We all needed to demand truth and action from the government.

It's not just about the environment. It's about everything. It's about existing. I, after all, am an existentialist. We need absolutely everybody on board. Life depends on it.

In May of 2019, Greenpeace, WWF and XR Spain hosted a press conference establishing the Alliance for the Declaration of a Climate Emergency, which boasted over 200 signatories from every corner of the peninsula. The headline in a fractured Spain read, 'Great Spanish alliance to make this the legislature for a Climate Emergency', with a focus on how civil society set aside differences and rallied around a call for a climate emergency declaration.

This time we had made it to the big media outlets and headlines.

I thought, harmony will exist upon being united by an apparent indomitable challenge. A single, simple, common denominator.

Greta Thunberg, XR and their ilk were opening our eyes to it, stripping away our masks, laying bare our collective eco-anxiety. Also, our collective hypocrisy.

We watched as the skies of Sao Paolo, Brazil, went dark with the smoke of a fire-ravaged Amazon.

Ahead of the next rebellion, set for 7 October, esXcomunicaR wrote a letter to the head of Spanish security forces, the minister of interior, Grande-Marlaska. In the spirit of 'Ubuntu' (taken from the Zulu language and loosely translated as 'I am because you are'), we thanked the police of Spain for their active role in guaranteeing the safety of its citizens. We dared to apologize for the inconvenience of our protest, on the premise that we did what we did for their (as well as our own) children.

Only by thanking our previous or perceived oppressors could we liberate them from their shackles. The letter was an olive branch stuffed in the barrel of their gun. It was published across national media headlines, potentially reaching the eyes of even the most junior police officers. Action, reaction. It unleashed the ire of social movements who perceived the police as the enemy.

They are not. No one can be. We needed adversaries as much as allies. Not enemies. Though we somehow compete we are, and must be, on the same side.

It was November 2019 in Chile. Brutal civil unrest erupted from inequality, courtesy the implementation of the Chicago Boys' neoliberal policies. Thus, the CoP25 was moved from Santiago to Madrid at the last minute. Our Madrid. The rebellion was coming to town, just in time for Christmas.

At the same time began Black Summer Down Under. An unprecedented mega-fire that would decimate Australia's unique and legendary ecosystem.

In the midst of it all, Ro woke me up early one morning. He was staying with me as he had come to help direct the XR movement's collective communications during the climate fest.

'Nic, I have an idea,' he said. 'I know someone with a horse ranch outside the city. Why don't we hire a truck, shovel manure onto it, and dump it, outside CoP, with a sign reading "Dear Leaders, The horseshit stops here."?'

Why not indeed? So we did it.

In January 2020, Spain's Parliament finally declared a climate and environmental emergency.

As we had eased into the new year, a promising 2020, I had moved on to XR Global Support, charged with setting up a public relations (PR) shop. I had the brilliant Bev by my side. A cultural PR specialist, she had been swayed by fear for her teenage son's future and was eager to donate her craft to climate. Protest is art.

Back to scratch.

We spun spells together, her and I. First, a video featuring Joaquin Phoenix as a doctor performing open heart surgery on a dying patient – Earth. In another video, Whoopi Goldberg narrated a perfect, imagined world for children, who would never know fireflies, if humanity continued to do nothing.

We were onto something.

Then, the pandemic set in. Eerily, scarily, as lives were extinguished on the whim of an invisible creature. Like the fireflies, we lost our way. The collapse of normalcy had come too soon.

'Extreme violence has a way of preventing us from seeing the interests it serves,' writes Naomi Klein in *The Shock Doctrine: The Rise of Disaster Capitalism*.

Humans withdrew into lockdowns, and nature started its rebound. Governments took advantage of streets quelled by confinement and pushed through their questionable agendas.

Then Kenya (where I was born) came a-knocking. Fazeela and her Maasai partners reached out to us on a Tuesday. The Kenyan government was using the pandemic to block protests and limit meetings related to the 'expansion' of Nairobi National Park. The only wildlife sanctuary within a national capital. The powers sought to expand a luxury hotel and road infrastructure. The plans not only threatened indigenous livelihoods but would also cut off vital migratory corridors for endangered wildlife.

We conjured our magic, and the word spread. *Al Jazeera*, the *New York Times* and *Hope Magazine* elevated the voices of those affected. And wonder of wonders, the government not only dropped the projects but also bought additional land for the park as a result of the campaign.

Meanwhile, a cloud of locusts, a product of freak weather, slowly ate their way across Africa. You could trace the event to the same phenomenon which unleashed the firestorm on kangaroos and koalas in Australia.

Armed with pen and chutzpah, Bev and I became conscious of the power for good residing within all of us, if only we try.

Just direct your feet to the river bank you want to reach.

As the pandemic dragged on, XR Global seemed to lose its compass, tugging in every direction and none, achieving little, and dwelling in frustration. Stubbornly, egotistically, and stupidly I insisted on pushing past all the resistance. Bashing my head against the brick walls that confined me, I surged ahead. My passion for my mission was blinding.

Summer had set in, and income had run dry. Bev and I thought, why not just go with the flow? What if we followed the path of least resistance and offered up love for life to those who wanted it?

We directed our feet, and life took us to the sunny side of the street.

I took a dip in the Mediterranean Sea, as I watched the mountains around me burn. I walked out covered in soot.

We called it The Clima. A public relations not-for-profit outfit focused on democratizing media communications and shifting global narratives. A public affairs department for the disenfranchised and the voiceless. Our clients would be communities and wildlife on the frontlines of the climate and ecological emergency.

And of course, the planet. With our art at heart, the climate would be our guide. One small gig at a time, our little agency took modest flight. Liberation was exhilarating.

One fateful day, Ina Maria tapped me on my virtual shoulder. Just as Typhoon Goni, also known as Super Typhoon Rolly, the strongest landfalling tropical cyclone on record, slammed into the Philippines.

Ina, artist and daughter of an assassinated Namibian freedom fighter. I recognized my sister the moment she said hello.

'A Canadian oil company is conducting oil and gas exploration in Kavango, the north of my country. The river which gives the region its name, snakes its way towards the Okavango Delta,' she explained. I remembered the name with awe from the time back when my home was South Africa.

'Africa's last great oasis, custodian of our planet's largest herd of elephants, Kavango is directly under threat because of greed. Can you help me get them out?'

I rolled up my sleeves, and bolstered by the network I generated in the past couple of years, sought funding and hired a fantastic global team of four. With our heads down, we spread word around the world about what was going on in Namibia and Botswana. We gave Ina a stage and passed her the mic to speak truth to power, to the North, to the World. In one solid, beautiful song.

By July 2021, Europe was flooded and California was burning. What happens in Kavango won't stay in Kavango.

Ina. My soulmate, alter ego, darling, demon; we hold a mirror up to each other. We give each other voice and wings.

Did you know the trees in the forest talk to each other? They are interconnected by a vast fungal web called the mycelial network. If a group of trees on one side of the forest detects a threat, say for example, a pest, it can warn trees on the other side to begin producing life-saving hormones. Even some nutrients have been known to be passed from one tree to another. The interconnection strengthens the wood.

I met up with Ina a year later in Glasgow, Scotland, for the first time, at CoP26. Betwixt whiskey and bagpipes, we connected to the climate mycelial network, awed to realize we were not lone trees in a decadent forest. Though the political outcome was to be the expected list of underwhelming promises, I found hope in the knowledge there was an army of people who had made the climate emergency their all. And yet, it's never enough.

I don't know how it will end. Are we too late? Some would suggest so. Yet, hope springs eternal. And hope cannot mean we keep waiting, but rather act. Or else, we will not be.

Humanity's unique triumph lies in listening to each other, empowered by the sharing of knowledge and the coming together of the whole, as primal as the woods.

When did we forget to talk with each other?

Every passing year expands the list of hottest temperatures on record.

So, I continue trundling on, working on shifting conversations in the different corners of the Earth which compose my story. Unbeknownst to me where this will lead.

Yet when my dying day arrives and a child asks me what I did to save our lives, I will honestly respond, 'Everything I possibly could… I gave the very best of me.' It is my hope to say this on a green and living planet where elephants roam and summer days can be enjoyed outside, sitting and telling this and other tales, you see.

'Climate action in Spain', European Parliament. Last accessed on 30 March 2024. https://www.europarl.europa.eu/RegData/etudes/BRIE/2021/690579/EPRS_BRI(2021)690579_EN.pdf.

Dominic Kirui, 'Concerted Campaign to Protect Nairobi National Park', INDepthNews, 28 August 2020. Last accessed on 30 March 2024. https://indepthnews.net/concerted-campaign-to-protect-nairobi-national-park/.

Jeff Masters. 'Super Typhoon Goni slams into Philippines as strongest landfalling tropical cyclone on record', Yale Climate Connections (website), 1 November 2020. Last accessed on 30 March 2024. https://yaleclimateconnections.org/2020/11/super-typhoon-goni-slams-into-philippines-as-strongest-landfalling-tropical-cyclone-on-record/.

'A Planned Oil Drilling Project Threatens the Okavango Delta Ecosystem', Earth.Org (website), 17 November 2020. Last accessed on 30 March 2024. https://earth.org/a-planned-oil-drilling-project-threatens-the-okavango-delta-ecosystem/.

23

Razom (Together) We Win!

Svitlana Romanko

I HATE WARS. I WOULD NEVER HAVE THOUGHT THAT MILLIONS of Ukrainians would witness a real war. Since 24 February 2022 our people have been dying, killed, orphaned, tortured, raped. Cities were destroyed, and people became happy just to be able to survive with simple bread and water. People with no power in the freezing winter. People suffering because of monstrous dictators funded by oil, gas and coal, and people killed by a fossil-fuel war.

Two years of a full-scale war have passed, but I think for us in Ukraine it has clearly been a decade of fighting the Russian aggressor – since they invaded Crimea and Donbas. Globally, on the positive side, we also made progress in escalating the renewable energy transition. There is a flip side of this global eye-opening moment of breaking free from fossil-fuelled dictators.

Fossil fuel companies have made a killing in annual profits this year, but those profits came from the blood and suffering of Ukrainians, and people across the globe.

These companies are looters; they've made more profits than ever off the shameful human fossil addicted society that they themselves created, and their actions have led us to a crisis of climate, energy and peace.

A good friend of mine told me that he liked my angry campaigning and resistance during the war, and that it's probably something that I was made for. I hope I can be instrumental in ending this war too. Was I, and we, Ukrainians, all meant to end this war and stop fossil-fuel dictators forever?

Were we all made to stop fossil fuels forever, in every single part of the world?

As a daughter of my sovereign nation, I consider freedom and justice to be essential, natural human rights. I am ready to fight for them until the very end. We will put an end to fossil-fuelled dictatorships and win the war. It will be the beginning of the era of decentralized clean energy, which benefits everyone on the planet and doesn't harm the climate. I am not going to give up until we win. Whatever it takes.

I lived through a turbulent historical time – the time when Chernobyl exploded. The Soviet Union (USSR) was falling apart as its artificial might dwindled, and we had an oppressive Ukrainian president, which resulted in the Revolution of Dignity. This major event, to move Ukraine away from dictators and oligarchs, and towards a participatory democracy, brought about serious changes. We were young, ambitious, resilient, hungry for justice, and we were winning.

We grew up when the climate movement in Ukraine was gathering steam. In 2001, I was the only university law graduate in my year who chose to do a PhD in environmental studies instead of pursuing a solid corporate law career everyone at that time wanted to take up for the sake of good money. I think I always valued the importance of being free to tell the truth to people in power. Corporate life places limits on the people who choose it, but a life of activism is free from these limitations.

In December 2022, I received a Rose Braz Award for bold activism. This award is very dear to me. Before the war, I was working at the giant climate movement 350.org and the social-justice-oriented Laudato Si' Movement. In these roles, I spoke with people from the Global South daily, witnessing the awful hardships caused by the climate crisis, injustice and inequality. Those sisters and brothers of mine are suffering and dying from the impact of climate change and constant crimes of the fossil-fuel companies. It should be them who tell their stories at all these fashionable annual UN Climate Summits. Together, we can end fossil-fuelled dictatorships and conflicts everywhere on Earth.

If you look into the fifty-two countries in the world that are still led by fossil-fuel dictators or autocrats, according to me, three are in Latin America and South America, twenty-seven are in Asia and the Middle East, and twenty-two are in Africa. Just on scratching the surface of the tough history of the conflicts you will find that fossil fuels have funded every single one of these dictators. Fossil fuels have become weapons of mass destruction, but the rich of the world hadn't noticed until Russia invaded Ukraine.

In 2022, the full-blown Russian war, fed by dirty fossils, came to my home, my country – the second largest country in Europe, yet small in comparison to the enemy. Russia started its attempts to invade Ukraine sneakily at first, in 2014. As global leaders donned poker faces, this violence went largely unnoticed on the global stage, and world leaders continued to court Putin, in the hope of growing their developed economies with cheap Russian fossil fuel, on the backs of Ukrainians in south-eastern regions that suffered due to Russia's low-level but consistent violence. The developed world felt comfortable being funded by fossil fuels, emitting its giga tonnes of CO_2. But you can never trust a deal with the devil. It won't ever pay off. And it didn't.

The Russian war against Ukraine maximized the global insecurity in the face of an attack by the second and third largest global exporter of oil and gas, and sixth largest exporter of coal. Russia even established a national welfare fund worth trillions of roubles to financially prepare for the war. Ukraine is now working on draining it to zero. We need to end the fossil-fuel addiction feeding Putin's war machine. All investments in Russian coal, oil and gas must be diverted to a clean energy revolution and towards rebuilding a green Ukraine from the war rubble.

The promise of Ukraine's resistance to oppression must be recognized and supported by the entire world. The rebuilding of Ukraine should be the beginning of a global movement for clean, renewable and safe energy.

As I write, it has been exactly two years since we all woke up to the explosions following Putin's speech aired on our televisions on the evening of 23 February 2022. He was spouting insane imperialist claptrap, which reeked of the Soviet past. At that time we could not imagine the impending war crimes that fell upon Bucha, Mariupol or

Kherson. We could not have imagined tens of thousands would be tortured, killed and dumped in mass graves. Military horror has nothing to do with peace and climate, but thanks to our resilience and national spirit, we are still alive. And we are fighting back. Defending and prevailing. This is the only choice we can make.

I remember that morning of February 24, 2022, when the war began. My family was drowsy and shocked, and so was I, when we woke up to the explosions and saw the grey smoke rising from the airport. This was not something that you expected on a regular morning. I still had my coffee, but we immediately packed our documents, dried food, power banks and warm clothes. But we went nowhere. Our bomb shelter was the basement in our apartment building. We sat there for long hours with our neighbours, and I remember one boy aged three who constantly asked his mother, 'I am hungry, will this war be finished before dinner?' As that little boy soon discovered, it wouldn't.

I recall spending most of the first week of the war organizing the Stand With Ukraine campaign, with many brilliant campaigners from within the country and across the world. Many of them were friends, heroes of their local and international climate fights and networks. Shining stars in finance, grassroots, Fossil Fuel Non-Proliferation Treaty, faith, human rights, or carbon bombs campaigning. Many people I worked with were involved in the climate movement. These fantastic people volunteered overnight and over the next weekend to launch a global call to end the fossil-fuel addiction which fed Putin's war machine. We were the people of the global climate movement, and the passion to tackle climate change in the tough time of war brought us all together.

Our first op-ed with my friend Bill McKibben, a grand trailblazer of the climate movement, shifted sentiments greatly towards completely defunding Putin's war bankers.

Together we win. Together we stand. *Razom* we stand.

That week changed my life completely. In the framework of this campaign, a letter calling on world leaders to end the global fossil-fuel addiction that financed Putin's war was distributed. It was a huge success, collecting signatures from more than 860 organizations in 60 countries. This resulted in a further high-impact global campaign to sanction Russian fossil fuels, cease all investments in Russian energy infrastructure, and phase out fossil fuels globally. As a result of our organizing, and the passionate work of many, partners across the globe from the EU, US, UK, Canada and later other G7 countries sanctioned Russian coal and oil, and dramatically decreased their demand for gas. This campaign also led to a shift in narratives and paved the way for an effective embargo and sanctions on Russian fossil fuels and accelerated the renewable energy transition in the EU.

Razom We Stand was set up in June 2022, emerging directly from the Stand With Ukraine campaign as a new international Ukrainian organization. *Razom* is the Ukrainian word for 'together', and building upon the first campaigning successes with friends, it quickly became clear that by standing together we would reach our highest goals.

Our friends at Sunrise Project supported and inspired us to dare for more. Our main goal is to accelerate the

Ukrainian and global transition from fossil fuels to clean energy, while continuing to push for a complete embargo of the Russian oil and gas industry. The creation of Razom We Stand benefited from the strong support from and actions of numerous national and international strategic partners.

Our organization is now considered the leading voice against fossil fuel dictators and war profiteers and for promoting a clean energy revolution. We will further enhance and expand our activities in line with our long-term strategy. In particular, we will further support international efforts to drive the contraction and demise of the fossil fuel industry in Russia, to prevent its expansion elsewhere, and to build on the achievements of the Stand With Ukraine campaign.

Many days have passed since the war started, a lot of blood has been spilt, of those young and old, dead and alive, to save our country and fight the dictator. We dream of making Ukraine victorious as well as the first post-war country in a world where renewable energy is at the front and centre of energy policy and a key area for investment, displacing on a large scale depreciated or destroyed fossil-fuel infrastructure. Our goal is for Ukraine to become a positive glowing global showcase eventually for infrastructure-centred climate action.

There was a time in my career, after active and successful grassroots activism against Chevron, when I was actively encouraged by a range of political parties to campaign as a candidate for my local city council. However, activism is activism only when it goes along with freedom of choice and action. Though I wished in the Summer of 2022 to become an MEP (Member of European Parliament), preferably from the European People's Party (EPP). The EPP mostly greenlighted climate-damaging fossil gas (so-called natural) as part of the harmful EU taxonomy debate (effectively defining what was and wasn't acceptable as an energy alternative as a part of a just transition) within the European Parliament, with the help of our Ministry of Energy who through a biased letter blew up any chance of excluding gas as a transition fuel, backing gas and nuclear as a viable option for the future money flows. I wanted to be inside the European Parliament, to help put brakes on this insidious interest-driven political project that enabled the passing of this horrifying and deadly policy, so detrimental to any efforts to mitigate the climate emergency. It is my hope that voters will stop them in the next elections. There is no place in modern politics for people disrespecting and ignoring the climate and ecological crisis.

Now is the time for policymakers and powerbrokers to cut murderous oil, gas and coal money flows to Russia. Ukraine is already rebuilding its energy grid, and this should be done in a decentralized, sustainable fashion and be powered by clean energy. Putin has unwittingly distorted energy markets forever and forced through an acceleration of a just and clean energy transition. Global leaders need to bring renewables to their contributions and make Ukraine an example of the first country that won over fossil-fuelled terror and climate change, rebuilding without dirty energy while also hitting Putin, other petro-dictators and the oil and gas industry where it really hurts – their very future.

And the world will break free.

'Svitlana Romanko, Joye Braun Honored With Rose Braz Award for Bold Activism', Center for Biological Diversity (website), 22 December 2022. Last accessed on 30 March 2024. https://biologicaldiversity.org/w/news/press-releases/svitlana-romanko-joye-braun-honored-with-rose-braz-award-for-bold-activism-2022-12-22/.

Center for Preventive Action, 'War in Ukraine', Global Conflict Tracker (website), last updated 6 March 2024. Last accessed on 30 March 2024.

Afterword

Roger Hallam

SO, THERE YOU HAVE IT. THOSE OF YOU THAT HAVE BEEN paying attention – we are fucked. Someone just has to say it as it is. Like in a family row. Sometimes, you just have to have it out with those you love. Otherwise, what does love mean? Certainly not indifference. 'You are ruining your life, and well, that's up to you I guess.' That is not love. At least, if you are not part of the temporarily privileged Western middle class, and those that copy their ideologies.

Throughout history, humans have survived because of duty: the duty to love, to intervene. To say 'no' when the situation requires it.

It's the same with your neighbour, your tribe, your nation – humanity itself. Sometimes, you have to say 'no'. Not because it will work but because it has to be done. Because of who you are: a being embedded in this world. Without the world, you are nothing. As an act of faith, but no less important for being so. Some things, many things, if you are open to admitting it, are matters of faith.

For the past few years, I have been getting through four to five articles a day about neighbourhoods, tribes, nations – humanity itself.

What actually science is trying to say, at least to those that understand the notion of the duty to love is simply this: that what we love, our family, tribe, nation and humanity, are being and soon will be forever fucked. Let me put it this way: imagine a high fence a thousand miles long, across plains and mountains, as far as the eye can see. And on one side of that fence are millions of corpses – men, women and children – limp bodies, jagged limbs. We know what it looks like. We in Europe cannot turn away because it has happened before.

Except this time around, it will go on forever, until there are no more millions, or billions should I say to kill, to die. Limp bodies stretching out for miles and miles and miles.

Let me cut to the chase. Maybe the most important question of our time is this: where are the people of India going to go? The Bangladeshis, the Pakistanis, the Iranians when temperatures hit 50–60°C? When the wet bulb effect kills the body – every body – in six hours? It's a science thing, right? Like being shot in the head, like being drowned in the sea, like being trapped outside at night naked at –20°C. You die.

Sometimes, things are certain, and you ignore certainties at your peril.

Let me summarize my 10,000 hours of reading four to five articles a day. Over the following decades, one thousand million will be killed – that is twenty times more than those who died in the Second World War. Global gross national product will fall by 50 per cent and never recover. You're right, although these numbers come from peer-reviewed papers, they could be wrong. Which, to be honest, actually means they could be a lot worse. As a sociologist, I would say that because science exists in society and is thus subject to social influences – the conservative methodologies and political pressures – just about all the predictions are underestimates. Isn't the most common phrase in articles now, 'scientists were surprised that...'

To stop this horror of horrors, the world needs to reduce carbon emissions by around 8.3 per cent a year. During the COVID-19 pandemic, emissions fell by an estimated 4 per cent.

So, it is not going to happen. Not because it is not possible, but because it is not possible under the existing carbon regime – the present set of human-made political, social and economic arrangements. The situation can change, and it will change when the regime changes. And the name for that change is 'revolution'.

It is important to understand that revolutions are not, in the main, brought about by revolutionaries but rather by the elites in power who commit collective suicide. They decide to pursue courses of action that destroy their societies and thus themselves. They spend too much money, they engage in ruinous wars, or they destroy the natural environment – the source of all material well-being. They no longer can see reality.

The question then is not, revolution or no revolution? The question is what type of revolution: a reversion into the hell of colonialism, fascism and totalitarianism, our global history for the past few hundred years. Or something else – something new which is also very old.

You will not discover this 'something' by reading articles or books, not even this book or this afterword. Sure. You will read about solutions and plans and strategies on the page. But to be able to create a new world, to save those you love: you will only find that knowledge in the police van, in the prison cell, by passing through the long dark nights of despair. Only then you'd be presented with a decision to make: to act for God or act for yourself. There is no middle ground. It is a matter of faith. The way coming out of years of the French Resistance in World War II, the French had to decide to act for justice or act for nihilism.

I have chosen to act for justice. The key word here is 'act'. And you do not act alone – you act with knowledge. Action and knowledge are two sides of the same coin. The reason why the global climate movements have been largely unsuccessful is because they do not marry knowledge and action well.

When a scientist, politician, diplomat – all the representatives of the global carbon regime – tell you we are going over 2°C, and maybe that a billion people stand to die and do not raise their voice, do not tear off their tie in rage, don't spill tears of desperation, don't leave the podium, resign from their position, sit on the road and say 'never again'. When they do not find themselves put in a locked room... well you go back to what you were doing – like billions of others.

I have been arrested for resisting the mayhem in this world more times than I can remember. The last time was three days before writing this piece. I have been sent to prison three times in the past five years – the last time for four months for making a speech telling people what I am telling you now. I am to be sentenced for another 'offence' in a few weeks, so I may be incarcerated by the time you read this. You might need to know that I spent three years sleeping in my car and under my PhD desk doing the research that led to the founding of the Extinction Rebellion. I got suspended from my university and went on hunger strike to force it to take climate action. I got divorced so I can do this work. And I will be doing this work for the rest of my life.

What I have done and what has happened to me is nothing unusual. It is what happens when you act – really act – for justice. It is happening to millions of people right now, and hundreds of millions have struggled and died for justice in the last hundred years. This is what you need to do if you claim to love what you love and the people you love. It's time to look in the mirror.

I decided to write this text because my friend Chittranjan (Chit) said it would reach an Indian readership. I believe India is one of the countries that might lead humanity out of the abyss.

All I have written here is not new. I claim no originality. We will not learn from books but from love in action, from its agony and its ecstasy. The most important thing is 'self-purification' not the act of civil disobedience itself. Unless you understand yourself and the world, you cannot act in love, and you will just make the world worse. I am led to understand there are many in India who have turned about from such realities and are temporarily under the spell of Adam Smith – the idea that happiness is about accumulation of stuff. Of course, it is true enough, but it is now leading to hell. Because it is. Look up – look around you.

Which leads me to you and me now at this moment. I have tried to communicate that we are set within the world. There is no disembodied knowledge. You cannot sit down in a room and get the answers. But this is the conceit of modern academia rooted in Western 'rationalism' – that you write an article, you give information and argument, this is assessed (like a computer) and then people change the world.

The climate movements are rooted in this conceit. They are part of this global Westernized detached culture. It is self-serving as it avoids the necessity for commitment and sacrifice. It is, to be blunt, bollocks.

Having read what you have, you have to act. And you need to know concretely what to do. This text, this book, has to be committed and embedded, not in the comforts of intellectual gossips but in pathways to collective struggle.

Here is one. Come and join us, and you will meet people involved in some of the most effective nonviolent resistance all round the world. Then you can act. And isn't this what we are all called to do – the most we can do. Nothing more, nothing less.

I wish you all the best.

Gloria Dickie, 'Explainer: How is climate change driving dangerous 'wet-bulb' temperatures?', Reuters, 10 August 2023. Last accessed on 28 March 2024. https://www.reuters.com/business/environment/how-is-climate-change-driving-dangerous-wet-bulb-temperatures-2023-08-09/#:~:text=High%20wet%2Dbulb%20temperatures%20are,is%20around%2037C%20(98F).

P. Bhanumati, Mark de Haan, James William Tebrake, 'Greenhouse Emissions Rise to Record, Erasing Drop During Pandemic', IMF Blog (website), 30 June 2022. Last accessed on 30 March 2024. https://www.imf.org/en/Blogs/Articles/2022/06/30/greenhouse-emissions-rise-to-record-erasing-drop-during-pandemic.

'The Evidence Is Clear: The Time for Action Is Now. We Can Halve Emissions by 2030', United Nations Climate Change (website), 04 April 2022. Last accessed on 01 April 2024. https://unfccc.int/news/the-evidence-is-clear-the-time-for-action-is-now-we-can-halve-emissions-by-2030.